UNINHIBITED

UNINHIBITED

DUANIA K. HALL

authorHOUSE®

AuthorHouse™
1663 Liberty Drive
Bloomington, IN 47403
www.authorhouse.com
Phone: 1-800-839-8640

First published by AuthorHouse   01/12/2012

ISBN: 978-1-4685-3893-9 (sc)
ISBN: 978-1-4685-3892-2 (ebk)

Library of Congress Control Number: 2012900004

Printed in the United States of America

Any people depicted in stock imagery provided by Thinkstock are models, and such images are being used for illustrative purposes only.
Certain stock imagery © Thinkstock.

This book is printed on acid-free paper.

Because of the dynamic nature of the Internet, any web addresses or links contained in this book may have changed since publication and may no longer be valid. The views expressed in this work are solely those of the author and do not necessarily reflect the views of the publisher, and the publisher hereby disclaims any responsibility for them.

THE BEGINNING

When most people hear the word UNINHIBITED they automatically think of wild sex, which is not a subject of opposition. Many have allowed themselves to indulge in the freedom that comes through the escapes that intercourse provides, but I want you to elevate your mind to think of the very things that you've indulged in that kept you from truly being free; be it a person, place or thing.

What has put a restraint on your expression, handcuffed your self-esteem, or vibrated your pain till you became numb to it's reign? What has gagged your confidence, whipped your manhood or womanhood like a slave being stripped of their very right to just be? What harness or rope caused your head to hang low? What swing caused your emotions to travel in deep circles?

What has seized your artistic virginity from its beautiful release, causing you to take off your dance shoes, block the melodies from leaving your vocal cave, let your paintbrushes dry, allow dust to collect on your camera till it looks like its been covered with snow that blocks the driveway of your visions, put your pen down, leave the stage, let the hot combs and curling irons grow cold, close your makeup kit, pawn your saxophone . . . abandoning any type of performance zone?

Was it that man, that woman, that mother, that father, that sister, that brother, that child, that job, that co-worker, that church, that rape, that abuser, that past failure, or that fear of criticism? Whatever IT was . . . . .Let It Go . . . . .Bury It and allow yourself to be **UNINHIBITED** in the things that God created you to do . . . as only you can.

Table of Contents

ARTISTICALLY
SPEAKING

The Tribute

To my Brothas and Sistas in Poetry,

All due respect for your variations of floetry. You speak and it causes me to grow and know; I have new levels to peak if I seek to leek God's reality. Stroking the mic with verbal penetrations. Prophetic power can't be faked and must awaken sleeping spirits; who aren't on the right track but are near it, and can reach it if they drop the fear. I got an inspirational twitch. There's **uninhibited** *deliverance in your words so slick. My hand starts to itch for its pen and then my thoughts roll in like tidal waves; just some nourishment from the energy feeding tube you gave, that helps me mentally runaway from the plantation of bullshit like a slave who found her freedom papers. You provided a home for my inner visions without the need of intent circumcision. Under the lights you see me and still let me be me. Yall be polishing the mic sorely. Lyrical pimps demanding increase of spoken currency. Don't mind being your whore overtime. Working every corner of lost minds so nothing learned via this expression is ignored. On a mission that will set others free, as your greatness goes before me.*

With Love and Respect,
Duania aka The Owner

Shades of Africa, The Poets' Jazz House, Word Play Live, Oralgasms, Still Waters, Boutique Divas Underground, Speak Out Loud, S.W.A.M., and Sankofa's Word

The Pledge

I pledge allegiance to Spoken Word
Of the poet's society of Amerikka
And to the founders for which it stands
One nation under God
Who gave US this gift of the tongue
Indivisible from our purpose driven reality
Exercising the liberty to "tell it" like it is
Fighting against unexcused absence
Of consciousness
And striving for self-love that transforms
To one love for all

Poetic Image

There's something beautiful about the imperfection of a picture that has captured a moment in time never to return

Something most intriguing about the allowance of a third eye that breeds life in ways that some can only or never dream of

Something sensual about what dwells
beyond the surface of a pupil

Something enchanting about creation
that is singled out through one human's perception

Something within this box that pushes
our mental abilities to the edge and
literally changes how we thought we used to feel

Something so mystical about a stolen space in time
that causes one to ask "Is this real"?

Something puzzling about the many pieces
that inhabit this which is saved on a negative
that shoots out a positive life form-
like a first born whose cry awakens the senses
of all those within range

Something spiritual about the journey an image takes you on that calms even the wildest beast within us

Something captivating about the many expressions of a child that stands as a caption of who they may become

Something political about the hierarchy of our souls
that decides which pose or prose gets overthrown
and those you deem as the one

Something poetic about photography
Inevitable relationship between unspoken and
spoken word as they both reveal a biographical outlook on the Creator's
subjects

Teachers of what life can otherwise bring to sodomy
Its growth won't allow for monotony but opts for tonal variations that
serve as markers for history in motion

True potion that frees what's inside of you
that which you hide in you
that which needs to breathe lest it die in you-
no matter which side of the lens or mic you ride it through

Euphoric manner of composition that
demands your values reposition
This art gives you courage
with no need for the liquid

It's readers are breeders of new readers who
are fortunate enough to encounter its 1,000 words

Agents of those whose situation yearns for broader investigation as
theirs are stories that need and must be told

Something extraordinary about this channel
through which the freedom of creativity
connects with the God in me and the God in you

There's something

ACKNOWLEDGE HIM

Good Morning Lord,

I am here to acknowledge your presence which I so often do not do at the start of my day. You declared me worthy of life once more, yet routinely I rise and begin my first breath with the worrying of the coming chores. Horoscopes have not the insight your relationship with the future entails; yet I hold a Masters in sleep walking for fear of those things at which I may fail. Tell me why I repeat this tortured meeting of both sides of my mind? Harder and harder I grind but a resting place for my wrestled soul I cannot find because I opted to follow the wrong mankind. Sequels changed my diamond status to a dime. In empty pockets, one could conduct an endless search for a treasure that even if full, was there never; because monetary value has no value in the spiritual world. You can't buy your way into Heaven, yet I scouted things that took me further away from He who created days 1-7. Lord I'm sitting here thinking about you like a woman who just met the man she knows is her forever. Through every endeavor, you have kept me even when protection was necessary from within. Lend me your continuous mercy when my eyes were blind and could not see that you are my constant. You go beyond all the nouns and verbs I've ever written. You love me without beats missing, like a man who is smitten over a dream he never thought would one day speak back to him. When you make plans to bless me it is more than just a Genie's bottle fondling ceremony. It is a gift designed for me only and it is better than anything I could wish, think, or feel. It's sealed with your divine stamp so I know it's Real-ly the moment you allowed to occur despite countless detours. You've loved me in a way that makes no sense as I have yet to create a twin love of its manner . . . banner over me . . . no conditions required. A rechargeable battery of no turning back with me. Free is how you intend for me to be, but I switch things up like Jonah. Sometimes I think I know what's best for me or truth be told, just too scared to give the rest of me—not understanding that withholding has been holding me back. So I'm ready to come out of the belly of the fish. Jeremiah told me that you have plans for me. The perfect fate that will literally change lives on different dates, mine included. So how do I get back to where Adam and I were rooted? Lord I love you but I do not always behave in ways that speak this truth. Sorrow precedes

me with thoughts of breaking your heart with matching pieces of mine. It's time to stand firm in this. No more wiggling worm with this. You are the epitome of bliss. Original poet who pours the rain and shines the sun for me. Pleas of forgiveness in doses that are high. To you, myself, no longer will I deny as you give me no less and there is nothing or no one comparative to your best. I've got on my good shoes, purchased for my run back to you. Grace told me your arms would be wide open and hug me tighter than ever before; to secure me of what I've forgotten along the way. You promised to NEVER leave nor forsake me. BUT I was always the one to dance the prodigal routine as you stood still while I worked out my "Human Being" thing. Pre-ordered was my return. Many third degree burns from paths I've chosen and yearning for them I put on frozen, with no defrost option. I put full trust in you who can stop them. Someone once told me that you must earn and learn your mate. Your love don't cost a thing but I misunderstood the importance of getting to know you as well as you know me. Revelations states that you are not big on material things. Your heart receives joy from the obedience I bring. Can't obey you without understanding of your Word and the desire to follow it; so I'll have the main course of your Word, getting second helpings to not only chew, but also swallow it.

Sincerely,
Your girl

More than Words

Been going through hard times
And I raise the praise
Devil thought he had me but it was just a phase
You have never left me and said
My blessings weren't denied just delayed
Went down the forbidden path
Now another road for my spirit you repaved
I prayed for you to create in me a clean heart
So I could walk this earth
With you shining through every part
Poetry leaves my tongue as a ministry
Sharing "How Great Thou Art" and
Releasing the hope that you've given me
So many people feel their lives
Have lost its very meaning
I stand here today as a symbol of your grace
That breeds redeeming
In the midst of darkness this soul is still on fire
Your Word is true and when death came knocking
You said no I'll take her higher
Those who don't really know you
Speak against you as deniers
I'll change their verdict with my testimony
Wear your mercy like a flyer
Standing as a witness of you almighty King
You are not just amazing and excellent

Lord you are EVERYTHING
With You before me I've got nothing worthy to lose
Perform spoken word like you do miracles
So around the world the gospel will be fused
I'll sing
I'll Dance
And whatever else I can
Cause you not only kept me
But mapped out a righteous plan
Daily my life extends my love letter to you
To express what you are to me
Words alone just won't do

DNA

Need You

I need you in this moment when everything is alright
I need you to permeate my intellectual atmosphere
While my children are sleeping tonight
I need you to nurse my wounds from
The day that is already done
I need you to prep me for wounds
That will greet me with the next rise of the sun
I need you to talk to me about troubles of
Which even you have to vent
I need you to reassure me that as a solid oak tree
I won't break although I get bent
I need you to allow me to sit at your feet
And listen to past stories you share
I need you to rub me with the oils of your confidence
So that I can be naked without feeling bare
I need you to massage my temples till they release
All that is not in line with being your temple
I need you to realign my pattern of thinking
To a mode that is pure and simple
I need you to gaze into my eyes
Causing me to undoubtedly know who you are

I need you to serenade me with slide shows of
How you've had my back thus far
I need you to fill me with all that is your essence
I need you to saturate my spirit so that you leak
Whenever others are in my presence
I need you to be real with me about
Times ahead that mirror hard
Then let me be real with you about
Times when I further extended my guard
I need you to hug me till dismissed are my fears
I need you to calm my inner storms with
The whisper of scriptures in my ear
I need you to provide answers to
Questionable things in my past
I need you to give full description of my home
That will outlast this earthly way station-
That often is a reflection of segregation-
As I feel its offerings keep me away from you
I need more times like this for US
So our relationship can be renewed
Lord I need you

My Love for You

Expanding my view of you-
The size of your greatness has no measure
I find new pleasure in sitting quietly,
Waiting to hear your voice
The day begins and
I rejoice at yet another chance you've given me
Daily escaping this world's trivia by
Soaking in a bath of your forgiving love
Raindrops of your essence pour down from above
And leave me in awe-
Thru you I saw life in a whole new way
Unfaithful to you with remnants of pain-
Could never gain the orgasmic sensation-
That comes from a relation with you-
Almighty King
Crazy enough I've journeyed through life,
Leaving you behind-
Thought I could **B.O.S.S.** up if I did my own thing
Sins tarnished the ring you gave me at birth but
Your romance is so infinite, you restored me-
With the origin of your worth

I've searched and not found a touch like yours-
That astounds my body's frame
The hottest track gets produces
When you say my name
Never the same, cause you removed my shame and
Made my slate again, plain
No longer thirsting after seals of others approval-

To experience fame
Want to get back on the right team-
Before I finish this game
Talents even unknown you've deposited-
So greater I could be
Had to shut my hearing OFF to those who said-
You were just not into me
You loved me past my pains
You are my symphony
I desire to issue a return as I've learned-
That you will never leave me-
As forsake exempts your vocabulary
I lay ALL of me under a pillow so you can-
Recycle it like the tooth fairy
It gets scary out here on this mission but
For every bruise I get, your Word issues a kiss-
Of promises that cannot be broken
Just a token of what you have in store for me
Virtue is restored in me
Buried the devil's whore in me
Reviving others with reflections of you-
That's the way to really score
Start taking less and giving more
I anticipate the day when you invite me to-
Walk through your front door and kick it with Angels
With wings like the Eagle, I now soar
Back in the day I didn't even believe I could fly
Now I open my eyes and have a box seat to-
Your mansion in the sky

Father you loved me when-
I couldn't stand to even look at myself
NOTHING and EVERYTHING because of you
You are my greatest wealth
Slide shows of my past bleeds the reality of-
How you always wanted me-
Even suffered and died for me
I put my own chains on when the cross had-
Already deemed my slave free
Took the speck out my own eye and
Hold the papers that declared-
The freedom that I've been yearning for-
Was always right there
You numbered the very hairs on my head
Like the lame, you told me to rise from-
My self pity and take up my bed-
And walk the line to a time when I would-
Transition from, X-rated or People-rated-
To God-dated Victory
Chosen to make History
Sharing with the world His story
That can change their story to-
Rich not poor, The Head and not the Tail,
Above and not Beneath
You put me back together again and
For that I'll always speak without a peak-
Watching your glory leak as the world reeks-
Of continuous resurrections.

Who You Are

In the game lames scout out blind fame
Looking for a donkey so they can pin the blame
Devil caught his own reflection-
Started feeling paranoid
Hour glass turned down
All bets are void
True soldier with so much weight on my shoulder
Haters trying to erase what God put in my folder
Spreading rumors through My Space-
Taking shots so cheap
Satanic frogs I watch you leap
You judge my past but God judges my heart
Command light to come forth when I'm in the dark
Those I was loving turned narks of the street
Teaming up with other lost sheep-
To map out my defeat
They just gave me extra wings-
To finish out this thing
I have specific orders from the almighty King
Elohim, Elshadi, my Jehovah Jirah
Still moving and shaking cause-

God is my provider
True Gangsta
I don't claim Blood or Crip
Nominated for salvation not just one hit
You should've known better than to
Try to flip my script
Cause I'm the true story-
Spoken straight from the Master's lips
I was born with prophet scars
Gifts of the tongue seem so bizarre
In the ring with the devil
Won every spar
I've come to show them who YOU are

My Lover

Like the sparkling waves of the deep blue sea
The love of only one flows unconditionally
More amazing than a 10 carat ring
What compares to him?
There is nothing
What he gives is better than S-E-X
Has the affects of a hex
Changed my walk, changed my talk
Attitude no longer rude
His affection strips me of
Insecurities formed with other dudes
He showers me with the
Fragrance of forgiveness
Said I'm a queen and
Should only accept royal business
His spiritual side is so good I cried as I realized
This lover didn't want nothing from
Between my thighs
Instead he chose to look me in the eyes and
Stare me into a convincing awareness of
My inner beauty
He's the real one you see
He's not the same
There's no shame in his game and
He never gives me a reason to blame him
For anything but his goodness and mercy
What's his name?
Denzel, Idris Malcolm or Todd
NAW
My lover's name is God

Where Would I Be

If it had not been for the Lord by my side
Where would I be?
If it had not been for the Lord by my side
Where would I be?

He covered me
From dangers I could not see
I was in the face of death
But he didn't let his angels rest
He thought I was worth saving
Despite all my sins
He's greater than all my strife
I'm so glad He's in my life

If it had not been for the Lord by my side
Where would I be?
If it had not been for the Lord by my side
Where would I be?

Tsunamis and hurricanes
Destruction at every turn, life is not the same
So much pain, feels like I'm going crazy
And my Christian walk has become lazy

But God sent His son to the cross
So my soul would not be lost
I've got to strive to live right
So I'll get a ticket to the next life

If it had not been for the Lord by my side
Where would I be?
If it had not been for the Lord by my side
Where would I be?

Where would I be, without the G?
Where would I be, without the G?
Where would I be?

1 Corinthians 13:4-7

Love suffers long and love is kind
Paints like a spiritual Picasso
In the corners of my mind
Does not parade itself nor does it envy
Gives wings to the things
I didn't know were within me
Love does not seek its own and is not provoked
My platform of courage no one else can revoke
Love thinks no evil nor rejoices in iniquity
Love works over time to bring out the best in me
Always keeps it 100 and rejoices in the truth
Is my shield when the devil and man get in cahoots
Love bears, believes, hopes and endures all things
Love declares reality from the pieces of my dreams
Rode the merry-go-round of self-destruction
And love was my bail
Said my destiny was beyond the White House
Not in the cell of a jail
Love has freed me and to it I say all hail
Love . . . . REAL love
Never-Ever Fails

The Way You Love Me

We go through this life looking for something special
Someone to love us just the way we are,
With all our flaws
On this endless search
For the greatest lover of all time
Not realizing, we don't have to seek
Cause He's there to find
He's everything that man could never ever be
I don't know what I'd do without Him and
The way He loves me

I was abused and confused so flesh I'd choose
Not understanding,
I had allowed my temple to be misused
My feelings went unspoken cause I was so broken
It wasn't real love, it was just a selfish token
You came along with a brand new song-
Cause my past was lived wrong
You said that it's okay, you came to stay
And love me in a brand new way

The way that you, you love me
The way that you, you love me Jesus
The way that you, you love me
The way that you, you love me Jesus

It's just the way you love me Jesus
It's just the way you love me Jesus

The way that you, you love me
The way that you, you love me Jesus
Jesus
Jesus
Jesus

Can Get Right

We know that He is worthy
But are you worthy-
Of the blessings that you ask for?
How many times has He come to visit and
You've not answered the door?
If there was a scoreboard of-
The life you lived for Him,
Would the opposing team have more?
Truth be told, I know at times my actions-
Have made His heart very sore
Positioned above and not beneath-
Is what He intended our lives for
But we keep insisting on using our own manuals and
Cry out when our souls turn up poor
For each one of us He gave that which was His only
Yet we sacrifice everything we have for
Some trick named Trina or some pimp named Tony
Saying we believe in Him with deepest love but
Spend no time which makes us phony
Perfected grin to accessorize our church dress
And match our suit and tie
Think we're fooling Him as we exercise living a lie
Keep going around in circles-
Searching for answers everywhere but in His word

How arrogant of us to allow dust to collect on it but
When hard times come we want to be heard
Shooting 3 pointers with our nice deeds-
Here and there
Or making touch downs with a great sermon
Up in the front of the class but belong in the back-
Since we've obviously not grasped what-
Past experiences should have us learning
Burning in my spirit for many short comings I've had
Tears streaming down cause-
Nothing is gained for telling God "Oh my bad"
Sad is the way we take advantage of Him
Causing our self and
Those we've been put in charge of-
To miss out on the True "high life" cause-
We keep jonesing for more sins
When will the pain be great enough for us to say-
'Enough is Enough and-
To our own vomit, never return?
If you want to see something better happen-
In your life;
For the things that encompass-
The heart of the Savior,
You must yearn

Earn your spot on the right team today-
For tomorrow hasn't made a promise yet
Haters count on you screwing up and
Have poke-her parties just to place their bets

Reset your mind and in turn reset your life
End your relationship with evil and
Change your name from-
Can't to Can get right
Daily entering this fight so put and
Keep God's armor on
Take your eyes off the water walker for too long and
All the numbers of your days will be gone
You can't do nothing about your past mistakes,
Except turn them like a key
Imperative to the future of others is that you take on-
Your purpose driven responsibility

It takes a village to raise the next generation,
So all young people should be viewed as kin
Show them a better way cause the world's ice-
Upon which they tread is paper thin
Begin to release your mind from the syndrome-
"Woe is me"
It's time to let go of what you were and
Embrace who in the beginning,
God said you would be
See there's no more time for screwing around
And playing games
Get back up again and start living a life that says-
Jesus didn't get His ass whooped in vain
Shame you holier than thou Christians-
Are tripping cause-
I just used the word ass
Spending too much time on judging people-
Is what got the church messed up fast

Stop smoking on that religion and
Take a hit of this here spiritual
When you accept others the way Jesus did-
You are bound to see a miracle
Whip your life back into shape,
Like every two weeks on your hair
Take the road less traveled and you will get there
Share the goodness of the Lord and
All He's brought you through
This glimpse into your life,
May influence what the next man-
Will or will not do
Chew on God's word like that gum,
That never loses its flavor
Represent Him like a tree that through any storm,
Will not waiver
Traitor you may be called by many-
Once you announce-
You won't get down the way you once did
Tell them to pucker to the cheek of their choice Cause-
No longer will God's will for your life be hid

Coming Back

Just another backslider
Sitting in the pew
Hearing songs and sermons
But still run from you
Singing with the praise team but
Each note becomes a strain
Pain surpassed my focus,
So my worship is in vain
Chaos in my life-
Makes it hard to keep on keeping on
Feel the sunrise is sure to bring a greeting-
From something else gone wrong
My spirit sleep walks-
In search of all that's missing
Needed some direction but
To which voice do I listen?

I'm coming back
Coming back to You Lord
I'm coming back
Coming back home, where I belong

How did I get here-
Caught up in the rapture of sin?
Making bad decisions,
Out doing dirt
Messed up so bad even my reflection hurt
Confusion twisting my insides in knots
Choir began to sing the song,
God Has Not Forgot
Moving closer to the alter,
So I know I'm in the right spot
Hands lifted high and trying to remember,
How to make by knees bend
Don't have no rehearsed prayer,
Just need you to make me over again

I'm coming back
Coming back to you Lord
I'm coming back
Coming back home, where I belong

My Next Move

Don't care how long I have to crawl,
How brisk I have to walk,
How fast I have to run,
Which hills I have to climb,
Or what valleys I have to bind-
So long as we are intertwined, JESUS
I want the salvation you say is mine
Time has put out its best of tests
Many nights I wrestled from no rest-
Wishing that Raid would work on the devil,
Cause he was bugging my thoughts-
Like an infest of pests
Blessed is exactly how I did not feel
While that may sound wrong-
I've got to keep it real
I had a daily double struggle-
Over things which had not yet healed and
Its often a sight that sores eyes-
When what's underneath Photoshop is revealed
In the shower trying to wash off my sins
Figuring a good hour would make the perfect blend-
So that others wouldn't know precisely
Where I've been,
But the perfume of my impurities is hard to contend
So now a desperate ear I lend to you-
The one they say is closer than a brother or
A best friend
For such a time as this, your only son, you did send And
What I couldn't have predicted in this moment,

He already did defend
Now just like the father of the prodigal son,
Your arms stretched open when I thought you'd be
Done—Showing how your love . . .
Doesn't operate the same,
As men of my past
It's made with special ingredients,
That won't let it be cast-
By the irons of any fire
Committed to a mission to take me higher
Opening my eyes and see the devil is a liar
But never worked alone

He had help from those I tried so hard to trust-
Because he knew who I was meant to be
His deepest fear wasn't my inadequacy
He dreads the day that I look in God's mirror and
Return to my knees
So here I am Lord to say my vows to you-
Once more,
But not the same ones as before
You are the true love that I've been searching for And
Actually what I'm made of, right to my core
Come before you to learn how to be-
What you say I am
Nothing without you is my
(from this moment on) plan
Traveling with a new band, with new members Cause-
I must disconnect from those who keep asking me-

To do the 'old' dance, or poem, or song,
It's all wrong
And prolongs me stepping into the full purpose-
For which I arrived on earth
Not near a body of water Lord so,
I just humble myself at your feet-
In need of a new birth
Great worth you placed on me-
Through your sacrifices
Now I want your will more than mine
No matter what parts of me you have to slice;
I trust you to take those pieces that are broken
And make me a vessel;
Reaching those of varied language-
As now through you all my words are spoken
Licensed for trips beyond my imagination and
No sinister token can revoke it
OHHH I lay before you naked as there is-
No advantage to be taken from me
I rid myself of earthly garments of shame . . .
That were gifts-
From those who hoped I would never-
Take on the posture of a tree
Thee is to whom I surrender my ALL-
As opposed to lose
Sit quietly with Faith-
Until you show me my next move.

Just Be

Sitting on the couch at the crack of dawn
Sure to say good morning Lord
With the Y of my first yawn
It's still dark as the sun has not brought itself to rise
Submitting myself to your presence
And felt so much peace I began to cry
See when I come before you,
There is no need-
For a script or a dress rehearsal
You lay out a welcome mat
That couldn't be found anywhere universal
Unlike when I go out, to you, I come by myself
I leave BeBe, Prada, and Gucci in my closet and
Tell my fragrances, my wigs and my home girl MAC
To just chill on the shelf-
Cause my nudity is the real wealth
With you I know there's no impression to made
Just a humbling of my spirit-
Cause later will come something
That will put me in a position to need a save

On bended knees with hands stretched out
Able to close my eyes-
Cause hurting me aint what you're about
No worries of you trying to blue/black my face
Nor covering my mouth so
No one can hear me yell rape
No awkward moments of an unsuccessful first date
No ears left swollen from the gossip of "friends"
Who betray your trust and negate whatever you-
Thought you had over the years
NO

Fears do not attend our rendezvous
I don't wreck my brain trying to reach perfection-
Cause in your presence
Flows a constant resurrection
You allow me to say what's really on my heart
And mind;
Things that I couldn't say in front of others as
Repeats of criticism and crazy stares-
Is all I would find
In your presence is a reenactment of—
A swimmer diving in an ocean that is deep
They go down real low but
Come up higher than they started-
Because it's you whose promise did keep

Crawling to you on a regular-
Cause I need my fix of free
No fronting, No worrying, No being paranoid,
No being annoyed, No being toyed,
Simply overjoyed

Walking back to you on a regular-
Cause I need my fix of free
No mental frying, No lying and No inner dying
Cause with you there's constant relying

Running back to you as I need my fix of free
That can only be experienced in the comfort of you
Cause with you I can JUST BE

Need to Get a Piece

It's 4:03am
And I'm sitting here
Just waiting for you to touch me again
Desperately in need of a lend-
Of a piece of your peace
More than 7 times I've fallen and
Trying to be celibate from former sins
Been experiencing some hard times,
Because back to them I revert
Built in system of what was rooted in me-
From childhood,
Set off an alert
In the corners of my house-
For you, I search
Perched on the window sill of appeal
Cause in this moment it's you I need to feel
Yes, I have the option to fall into the arms-
Of another man, which could suffice
But I let a man touch me once before
And it came with a high price-
Especially after I let him do it twice

Gained orgasms in multiple cycles
Delusions of the path that led me-
Away from being your disciple
Limped back like a cat,
Who had been in many fights
On my 9th life and surrender myself to-
The seduction of your forgiveness by candlelight
Right is the way I'm trying to go
Can you whisper your poetic promises in my ear,
As I let my tears flow

NO-body can do me like you do
Painful passion in motion
Cause I need to get a piece of peace from you
Let us bathe together for some hours
You take your bar of Grace and
Cleanse me beyond my physical,
Then rinse off all those things that-
Caused me to be a coward in the spiritual
No pretense that you,
I have always properly "repped"
But now I seek admission
For submission of your will-
Cause me you have always kept . . . wet . . .
With the moisture of a true Father's love
Waxing me with movements
That didn't require a 'glove'-
That might not fit
Or choose to quit it's duty of protection and
Leave me pregnant with despair . . . NO
You are the one whose gentle touch
Always reminds me-
That I'm never left alone out 'there'
So in the dark for you I plead
Humbly down on my knees
Opening my mouth wide so that-
My tongue can release affirmations of repentance;
While your peace cradles me into the unknown zone
Sweet release confirmed by our synchronized sighs
The bond of the Shepherd and the Sheep
Cannot be denied

Appetite turned off for what the world offers me-
By the slice
Following my soul's compass-
Cause I need to get a piece of your peace tonight

LIFE LESSONS
PART I

For A While

What can I do?
I'm only a child
The derailing of my innocence
Has been going on for a while
I want to go outside and play Hopscotch
Or Double Dutch with another
Instead I watch in fear
As you put on a rubber
Lover of yours I became and
After each time you'd remind me
Not to tell anyone
About our little game
I began to make up stories
To lessen the suffering
When it was my turn
Maybe if I formed my lips just right
The "hotdog" would release its pressure
And a few hours of sleep I could earn
Then I'd dream of eating ice cream
Or playing Barbie dolls
Or even going to an amusement park
Until the next duty called
What can I do?
I'm only a child
I wish I could really be one
If only for a while

Cheers

If only you had let me know
That your love for me
Was merely touch and go
"I love you"!
"I want to spend my life with you"
These are the words
I heard constantly from you
And I was the fool
Who believed they were true
I've been caught up
In the rapture of pain
Cause I gave you my sunshine
And you gave me rain
Go ahead
Get one last tug at my heart
As things stand now
WE-MUST-PART
There's one more thing
I must come to realize
And believe me, I do
The fact is
There will be another life
Oh yes
After you
So cheers to the afterlife
Bartender of life
Fill my glass
And make it last!

Miss Lynwood Pageant (Back in the day)

Free?

What makes me free?
Is it merely because
I don't have any shackles
Or chains wrapped around me
What makes me free?
Is it because
I can come and go as I please
What makes me free?
The fact that I can choose
What it is I will become
And whose I will be
What makes me free?
Is it merely a state of mind
That no man can steal away
Is it my resistance
That keeps me from being enslaved
By this sick world's trash
In the form of a treasure
What makes us free?
Is it just because Jesus who never fails
Endured the pain of the nails
Is it because of simple belief in oneself
That saves you from insecurity
Is it the ability to loosen our shackles
By tightening someone else's noose
What makes us free?

Within the Clouds

Hit 3 bottles of Strawberry Boone's Farm
2 Paul Mason And 1 ½ of Alize
Determined to drown the memories
Of the coming holiday
A day that used to encompass
The building of memories
Surrounded with loved ones
And lots of good food to eat
But this year would be very different
As the dinner table will have 1 less seat
A headache and I woke up in the bathroom
After praying to the porcelain gods
And running up the water bill
The results of all I'd done to rid my soul of
The aching it continued to feel
REAL is the fact that
During certain holidays or seasons
There are some who have reasons to cry
Instead of laugh out loud
This would be a very hard Mother's Day
For me, as I looked to mine within the clouds

Note: This was my first Mother's Day without my mom (Jeanne Kay Hall) back in May 1994. **Stacy,** thanks for calling my daddy. **Daddy,** thanks for not letting me drive drunk, although I was quite determined to go out and party my pain away. **Mommy,** the way I miss you is beyond any poem I could ever write. I pray you are at peace now.

NIGGA PLZ
Part 1

Oh Really!
Yo no providin gas and
Hangin out all night ass-
Wanna drive my car?
You got a betta chance-
At seeing a shooting star.
WTH (What the hell)!
You ran out of minutes-
So you wanna take my cell phone?
You must be in a bad area cause-
Yo voice is startin ta roam.
Ooh you got a PhD (Pretty hard Dick)-
But sadly it matches yo hearin-
Cause stupidity in this relationship,
You keep tryin to instill and
Uh, Check this out-
I aint—that girl—no more!
This woman no longer shops at da
Rent A Sorry Ass Mutha Fucka **Center!**
Steve Harvey's book peeped me-
On da game of yo gender.
Caution: this truth may put a dent in yo ego's fender
You fired as my fake love lender!

NIGGA PLZ
Part II

Swamped with emotions that could-
Fill up seven seas
It's fucking tiring always trying to Nigga Plz
It has symptoms just like a disease and
If you don't catch it early-
It will spread like cancer seeds
Niggaz always come crying to you-
After they done something ignorant
Then you be working over time-
Trying to help with the figuring-
Of how to turn their mess around
Then you spend more years with-
The same ole same goin down
Sound off 1-2-3-4
Plzing this Nigga and that Nigga-
Is a job with no benefits and
They always keep asking for more
DAMN!
So who's the bigger Nigga?

Check The Tag

I determine what I'm worth and
How I am to be perceived on this earth
A true Queen inherits value from the moment of birth
No time to be wasting on jerks-
Who think they can gain ownership of my "jewels"-
With their smiles and perks

Did it ever occur to you Sir,
While you're dreaming of working your swerve
And hitting some genital nerves;
This body might be the storage of-
More than just curves?

Someone's **O**nly **U**nique **L**ineage-
That is in direct connect to the creator
Surely **O**f **U**nordinary **L**ikeness
Simply **O**ptically **U**nashamed **L**anai
Supernatural **O**mnipotent **U**mbilical **L**asso
Yes, a **SOUL**

What brought on your misplaced confidence-
Allowing you to drift in my direction?
Was my body language or attire-
Overemphasizing a need for affection and
You mistakenly thought I was only good-
For multiple erections?
The dog in you has a familiar complexion

Oh I've been previously acquainted-
With your species
Still searching for the manufacturer of the spray-
To rid my spirit of its fleas
I'm suffering like I have a disease!
The Desire to Please
But to that I must say at ease and
Place unhealthy emotions on freeze

God's portrait of me was not made with fear-
But with a crown to adorn my head all year long
I hate to bust your bubble mister,
But you thought wrong

You can't bid on me
I've already been purchased from the throne

You must be sleep walking and need to wake up
To acquire something this valuable-
You need more than good luck
You think I'm just another "piece"-
You can get for a buck
Well open your eyes cause reality has struck

Save yourself from being put in-
The embarrassment bag
Next time you're out shopping-
Check the Tag
Precious Cargo
Prepaid by the Cross
Priceless

MIS-TAKEN

You need to take your hand off your back
You've mistakenly been giving yourself a pat-
As you thought you did a number on me
Yeah, you thought you took my free but see-
It had nothing to do with the magic in you;
Just through you the devil knew-
He could take us both down

In the midst of my fall I grabbed my roots
And called out "Jesus PLEASE get me out of
this mess I clearly put myself in"
Scorched but not burned from my sin
You just happened to pass me when I was-
Already going down the wrong road
Open to all possibilities of bullshit to unfold

You could have lured me with a-
Saltine cracker without salt
Stuck in a vault of confusion
I welcomed your intrusion
Verbal, emotional, and physical abuse was profuse

Encounters of terror were close enough to-
Increase the business of Angeles Funeral Home,
As morals roamed

The oral nature of intercourse was coarse-
Like black pepper . . . Incomplete at best-
As if someone else needed to finish the rest
Equivalent of a biscuit eating ceremony-
Without the proper sopping technique
So when reaching the peak of my disappointment;
I would decline and just take my turn as I learned-
I could only get what my imagination gave
The modern day national anthem of a slave

My inner being churned like milk that had gone bad
And I was once again empty-
From dealing with a wimp;
Who could only breathe by
Shortening the breath of another
True little bitch under cover-
As in Christ you are my brother

Always shrunk down as I'd forgotten how to stand
Accepted the halves that presented themselves-
As the whole of a man

Mistaken, sitting around with-
Your chest puffed up proud
But here's a public announcement-
Coming at you real loud
Mistaken, thought you could steal my joy
Mistaken, thought you could me destroy
Mistaken, stop high fiving yourself like that-
Cause God answered my call
And put me back on track

You running a relay-
With no one to pass the baton too
Turned to the devil and he said
"You on your own nigga . . . I don't got you"
You got your self in a screwed up situation and
Even though you tried to stop-
You actually sped up my graduation

Mistaken, you're shaken cause I'm awakened-
To exactly what I'm here for
Mistaken, as you watch God open many doors
And counting blessings becomes my new chore
Mistaken, are you tired of being the devil's whore?
Taking all the wounds in this war
Mistaken, take a minute to understand-
You are fighting a twisted battle and
Blind to the real plan

You're on the front lines-
Cause the destruction of you,
Was the true win
Now look who's in the lion's den
Left to fend for the same rights-
You thought you had taken
Mistaken

Time

Time is that teacher-
That unexpectedly calls your name
Time is a reservation-
That cannot be changed
Time is something that causes-
Restructuring of your mind's frame
Time is not dictated by the roll of dice-
Like a just for fun game
Time is not something that-
Must or will wait on you
Time is inevitable to reveal what is true
Time mismanaged is like fruit left out to rot
Time is a true reflection that will show you-
Where you are or what you aint got
Time is something more valuable-
Than all we strive to attain
Time is the evidence of great joy
Or immeasurable pain
Time is your best friend-
Till you reach the age of old
Time is a request for seconds-
When you haven't reached your goals

Watch Your Mouth

How many times have you wished-
You could rewrite a sentence at the;
Very moment it was leaving your mouth?
How many times have you wished-
You could make a joke disappear like;
Stains on clothes that just got sprayed-
With some Shout?
How many times have you pierced-
Someone's heart with phrases that;
Left nothing of substance to gain?
How many times have you prayed for God-
To erase years of residue from the words;
Of loved ones that filled you with pain?
The tongue is one of the most powerful tools
And one of the most slaughtering-
All at the same time
Its technique can cut you deep-
Or even blow your mind
The tongue is something to play with-
Yet nothing to play with

I now understand what the old folks meant-
When they said-
"You better watch your mouth"
What comes out of your mouth-
Can literally extend life or-
Issue a death sentence
Tearing down walls of insecurity or
Putting up more segregating fences
He Say-She Say has been the culprit of-
Broken friendships and broken homes;
All because some runaway nouns and verbs-
Were allowed to freely roam
Words are the ingredients of rumors
And rumors start wars
Holy with the <u>ly</u> left off-
Changes a Queens name to whore
If God is love then what did He-
Intend our mouths for?
Watch Your Mouth!
Little girl takes pride in dropping it like its hot-
Because too many male figures;
Always told her what she's not

Now she's finding comfort-
Around the arms of a pole;
That stands as tall as the father who-
Was never around to console
School counselor told her-
"You can forget about college;
Cause you'll never make it"
So she told the DJ to play track 4;
So that she could shake it
Not understanding that if she just-
Gave her emotional curses to God;
He would break them off-
With some high self-esteem;
So other sistas that came up behind her-
Wouldn't stumble over the likes of;
Radio disc jockeys who seek to-
Continue a legacy of demean
Watch Your Mouth!

Words are also spoken through actions;
So even without sound people's lives are-
Impacted and just a fraction of a gesture;
Can get positive or negative reaction
Just like playing jacks, we have to-
Keep picking up more pieces;
Every time we take our turn
Treating others the way we want to be treated-
Is a lesson needing to be re-learned
Carry yourself in the light of-
The position God said is yours;
So when others say the worst about you-
Their words will be like a bird without wings;
Never to leave the ground, let alone soar
We've all seen the famous words
"God grant me the **Courage** to-
Change the things I can,
The **Serenity** to accept-
The things I can't and
The **Wisdom** to know the difference"
Everyone must exercise their ability to listen,
Before speaking-
So more intelligence can be leaking and
Those in close proximity who are peeking;
Will catch the vision and on others,
Stop making verbal incisions

Today make a To Do List-
Of saying positive things and
Although you can't control others,
Better days you can bring
Watch Your Mouth!

Dark Clouds

Change is necessary-
But familiar is where we are consoled
Spinning on the same merry-go-round,
Hasn't reached the age of old
Hearts hanging out from a jacket-
Without any sleeves
Morals turned so cold we've forgotten-
What it feels like to breathe
Achieved a Master's in how to display-
A prominent façade
So far removed from the Spiritual-
When our names were called;
We started hearing God
Faithful in taking our vitamins of complaint-
With a full glass of why me
Blindsided by our own procrastination that-
Made a million dollar auction block of our FREE
Reading materials on how to work everything-
Except our gift of LIFE
Dark clouds in our heads of wishes that-
Misplaced the switch to the Savior's light

Devastated from our current state-
To the point of taking ill
Bypassed His instructions and
Got in line to ride the-
Do what pleases ME Ferris wheel
Still part of the lineage of Abraham-
So getting our inheritance-
Should be high on the To Do list
Self compromise is burning the ladder of-
Our family tree like a voodoo kiss
Sitting in a corner with repeats of-
Should've, Could've reminisce
Somebody told the biggest lie-
When they said ignorance is bliss

Painful Observation

Painful Observations
A.K.A. Constructive Criticism
I allow you to come in and
Mess up my natural rhythm
Body jolts from shock treatment on repeat
Scratching blood from my arteries
And rewinding my heart's beat
Look up to the Heavens
Waiting for answers to quickly fall
No moisture on my forehead
So I feel like Jehovah is ignoring my call
Thoughts are spinning
As I play my life in heavy rotation
Used a map that was leading me
Further from my final destination
Self destruction on the inside
Had me question if I was part Haitian
It's a hard ass pill to swallow
When you've screwed up God's creation
Purchased some new pencils but
The past just won't seem to erase and

I stood over my mama's grave to ask
How come she didn't school me
For a proper graduation
Picking up my 'pieces' one by one
Cause my life is dehydrated
From lack of elevation

Beat down from the heat of denial
That's boxing in the ring with the truth
Dying from the escape I need
From things that happened back in my youth
Raise my glass to the sky so the redeemer can
Replenish the juice of my soul
Got out the pity wheel chair
And transferred to a walker
As I rewrote my goals
Blessing that He's not yet through with me
So the battle is not lost
Revelation that it aint for me to fight cause
It belongs to the real BOSS

Bullshit had me going in circles while searching
Cause I overstand the possibilities of more
Came to see I had the max in Him and
Began to refuse the devil's chores
Restructuring my life around spiritual wealth
With a greater return than the fast track of whores
On bended knee with a purpose and
Embracing what He says I'm here for
Been put on the cover of the Enquirer
Even when I've kept my nose clean
Put trust in the Savior and stopped buying
Sell-out blow jobs from mere human beings
If you've had me from the back
Sorry to tell you that it won't happen again
Father in Heaven promised to give me a mansion
So temporary illusions
I no longer need you to lend

It Happens

Tell me this was all a bad dream
Tell me my destiny is a vision beyond
What I have seen
Tell me my life will become an amusement park
With a whole new theme
Tell me everything will work out because
Right now my hope is on lean
Depravation of joy
Yes my soul is feanin for a new season
Lord I need you to tell me
It happened for a reason

Father's day is painful to a <u>little girl</u>
Whose dad was never around
She couldn't point him out in a line up
Or the smallest dog pound
Longing to hear him say goodnight sweetie
But she never heard a sound
His missing hugs and forehead kisses
Have left her dumbfound

Here we go again with <u>Baby Mama</u>
Shooting bullets of **drama**
This man is just trying to be there for his kids
While other cats have to
Get hunted down like Osama
He searches for patience
To have negative thoughts resisted
But it's a messed up situation and
He can't get no help from the system

Woman wakes up again wondering
Why she's laying next to a sorry mutha fucka
To change her current visual she'd give
Her life savings down to the last buck
As she thinks of how he stepped to her
With what seemed loving and REAL
If she had a lawyer
She'd ask for compensation for this raw deal
So her broken heart could be resealed
She hung in there for the little ones
But for her remaining sanity
A **divorce** had to be done

Life just aint the same without my mother
Lord you took her from me even though
You knew I needed and loved her
Daily my heart aches from
The pain of her absence
My soul constantly bleeds from
Not having her interaction
Not talking to you for a year
Was my numbed reaction
Don't mean no disrespect Father but
She was my life's greatest satisfaction

Tell me It happened for a reason
Tell me you haven't left
Tell me there's a good reason why
Me and Jesus wept
Tell me this was all part of your marvelous plan
Tell me I can still reach out and
Unchanging will be your hand
Tell me you still love me
Tell me you'll give me what I need to hold on
Tell me you'll make me a testimony
Tell me ahead are brighter days
Tell me my agony was just a passing phase
Tell me what's up because in this moment
I don't understand your ways

Tell me one day you'll make it all clear
Tell me from more of this madness
I don't have to fear
Tell me again about my room
At your mansion in the sky
Tell me there's sunshine to replace
All the cries of my whys
Tell me the devil really is a lie
Tell me I'll be free before the day I die
Tell me
Tell us
All this happened for a reason

The Same Blues

Imagine the pain of a mother who loses a child
It must saturate her spirit and cripple her for a while
What about the mother who gives her child away
She broke her own heart is what many would say
What about the father who cheers her on-
As she proceeds with the emptying of their seed;
All so he can continue to live a life-
That seems to remain free
What about the whole extortion of abortion-
That has US selling our souls to the devil in portions;
Making us the modern day lynchers-
Hanging innocent babies with the very cord-
That was meant to feed them;
All cause we're too scared to breed them
Or to selfish to heed the call of
The consequences of our sexual deeds

This surgical procedure is not birth control
Today I represent the WAKE UP patrol
Cause we're playing God's hand in the game of life
And that is dangerously bold

We don't see how we're doing the Cha Cha-
With Lucifer;
Allowing him to turn our hearts cold
We don't see how we're patronizing-
His destruction business with all our morals sold
We've become a people no longer-
Organizing marches for the rights of others
But a people who don't think with the right head-
Once we get under the covers
We can't evolve but revolve around-
Our low self-esteem and misplaced egos;
That need to hide behind a lover
And do not care about-
The worth of the life of another;
As we sign on the dotted line-
So someone else can smother
Damn . . . the rubber broke-
So now you choke and
No longer want to be in the category of grown folks-
Cause grown folks-
Have to deal with grown problems

And make decisions for children that are unselfish-
Not choices that will rob them
I sob and come at you with this verbal mob-
Because to many of us have this option of abortion-
Twisted and are not on our job

See an option is-
One proposal to initiate overlooked negligence
An option is-
Only preparing tasks incapable of negotiation
And option is-
Only purposed through introduction of needs
But all options are not meant to be . . . entertained;
Especially when someone else's well being-
Is at stake, just so you can gain

Clinics and Mortuaries
Are playing the same blues
Every time you have sex
More than the obvious things you choose

The concern of the unborn is often minimized-
Because they are not yet seen
But if you borrow the heart of the Most High-
You can literally feel the presence of a human being
You can hear the cry of that boy or girl
You can hear his laughter or
Put a bow around her curl
You can see him attempt to walk
And hear her when she 1st begins to talk
You can smell the diaper that needs to be changed
You can taste the victory of his 1st basketball game
Or clap at her recital if-
You allow your imagination to get within range
All that may seem strange to some
But it's a true appeal
I learned the hard way,
Even though the fetus is only a couple months old-
It is still REAL

I'm not here to put you down or give you the blues
I can step to you like this because;
I not only tried on but actually wore the same shoes
Like many I was afraid to give birth-
Because I thought having a baby-
Would kill my dreams
Now more than anything I want to say I'm sorry
I asked God to put me in a secluded place-
Just so I could see my son or daughter's-
Would have been face
And apologize;
With every tear that falls from my eyes-
Leaving guilty stains that can't be erased
And will forever trace the infliction of my painful sin
Feeling perplexed as the lineup of dead beat dads-
And absent fathers is parallel to the one I stood in
See I had this need to be in control
And I thought I was until I got up-
From the surgeon's table in pieces
And was no longer whole

I wondered if I discontinued my highway to Heaven
I needed God's mercy and grace
To operate for my 187

Clinics and Mortuaries
Are playing the same blues
Every time you have sex
More than the obvious things you choose

When I was with that man it felt good
And every right spot he hit
But in reality I never thought about anything-
Except how all over me he bit and
Issued rewards to my clit
And the poetry my tongue wrote-
That got applause from his stick
Afterwards I wasn't asking but literally begging-
For God to be like a homeless junkie-
Who digs through all the treasures that I trashed;
Cleaning them off then repositioning them-
For something that will outlast

As I grasped the aftermath of my chosen path
And its emotional wrath
I knew that if I had one more chance
I knew that if I had one more chance
I knew if I had one—more—chance
To glance at the boxes that allowed me to-
Check a decision to give life or take it;
I would not be shaken-
But awakened and say-
I CHOOSE LIFE!
Because God gave it to me twice

Clinics and Mortuaries
Are playing the same blues
Every time you have sex
More than the obvious things you choose

Don't pretend your life is your own
It's just a lend from the throne-
To help make sure, in the wrong direction,
Others don't roam

How can we preach about saving our youth-
That are here;
Yet sign papers at the clinic that authorize killing-
The unborn just to cover our fears
The growth of our own race we abuse and
Decide to auction off the very future of our muse

Ladies, sometimes we are justifiably-
Hard on the fellas-
Who don't take care of their kids;
But abusing the fact that we can decide to avoid-
The same responsibility with abortion;
Means the same ways as them we live

Fellas, sometimes you accuse the ladies of-
Having an easy way out because they have-
More weight in choosing that rode
But trust and believe-
In their hearts they carry a very heavy load

I feel for the fellas who paid for an abortion-
Because they were lied to by some heffa;
They took out on a date
But you've got to replace your Trojan-
With a thinking cap or the repercussions;
You won't be able to escape
I feel for the ladies who did it because-
They were raped and
Wanted to avoid the vis-ion of their trauma;
Every time they look in the eyes of their little one
But I beg you to seek Him who for this very reason-
Sacrificed His only Son
He will heal all your parts and
Give you a brand new start

Clinics and Mortuaries
Are playing the same blues
Every time you have sex
More than the obvious things you choose

Today I need everyone to get a clue
The path that leads to abortion-
Is a responsibility of two

Our minds usually don't go past her orgasm
Or his nut
Making that "I'm Grown" decision to fuck
Then piss out positive results and feel-
SOL (shit out of luck)
And seek to pass the buck to the doctor at the clinic
Or be that nigga who knowingly asks
"Who's the daddy?"
Saying my name is 'Benit' and
I'm the master of the 'pull out' game-
So I aint in it
Want relief from burdens we brought on our self
The easy way out now becomes our top shelf

I came to speak to you from deep within
If this message isn't for you-
Then save it for a friend

Clinics and mortuaries
Are playing the same blues
Every time you have sex
More than the obvious things you choose

Abstinence, Safe Sex and Repentance,
Birth Control Pills, Rubbers and Diaphragms
Before you lay down again-
I suggest you have a plan

Abstinence, Safe Sex and Repentance,
Birth Control Pills, Rubbers and Diaphragms
For every child's voice that's already been silenced
Spread this message like a disease
And help heal our land

The Secret

Somebody told me a secret and
I can't keep it to myself
It is the epitome of wealth

The mind shapes what you perceive,
So you must exercise extreme caution-
Of the things you grieve
Oh what trouble on ourselves we do bring,
Not heeding to the fact that-
Our thoughts immediately become things
On the track of life you must take extra laps
And focus on your positive passions-
Cause that's what makes things happen;
So says the Law of Attraction

Thoughts are the engines of our actions
And the explanations for others' reactions
And the answers to the whys of how our dreams
And visions relapse and
You must understand that-
Things dance to the very rhythm of your magnetism
Positive or Negative,
It's all relative to why your natural high
And drive have now become celibate
Feelings are feedback-
Like a court reporter, they read back;
What you've told yourself in private
And could no longer hide
And now must conquer and divide it-
So in this world you can successfully reside

It's a damn shame
This game makes us lamely insane-
Not knowing how to regain;
So the same problems won't remain
Bullshit stacked and you get off track
Oblivious to the fact that everything you need-
For your journey's nourishment;
God already packed . . .
Within
Yet we still search
We don't identify with our power-
To reverse the curse
See you are the one that creates your own universe

And you're the potter of your reality's clay
So how will you start your next today?
The same old way . . . .
Will get you the same results
And mess you up like joining a cult;
So decide to revolt and cut the bolts off your spirit

If you stop feeding off gossip and
Take a few bites of-
The Secret
You might just meet the real you
The you that God intended you to be
The you that can set others free
The you that says forget what you heard-
Cause I'm alright with me
The you that is a decree of a better tomorrow
Be like Aladdin who asked the Genie-
For what he really wanted
And not the introvert who-
Accepts what others want to give;
That later leaves you taunted

See, the restaurant of life is owned by God
And divinity is your waiter
So now, not later . . .
Place your order for what you thirst
And see how it tunes in with your new song
And helps write the next verse,
Unrehearsed and retrieved from birth

Rub elbows with greatness and
Cut ties with fakeness
Don't delay or 2nd guess opportunity
Drawing from the well of ingredients-
Needed for your purpose
And expressing gratitude for countless blessings-
Should be your unity
Don't hesitate or time waste
With FAITH you must take the 1st step-
Before you see the whole staircase
Knowing that you'll be okay-
Because even if there are no more steps;
You can just build some new ones anyway

Don't let the residual outcome of your past-
Be the legacy that outlasts you . . .
Must be honest about the things that attract you-
As boomerang is in the mix
And its catch 22 hurts like the bite of a Bitch
Develop an attitude that will have the latitude-
To shift your energy
Then synergy will be a nationwide remedy-
Of greatness multiplied by infinity

What you visualize becomes the eyes-
That materialize the I can or can't pass this test
And holding negative things in your sight can-
Mess up even the best intention;
Not to mention,
Your mind and body are endless lovers
So when you put your mind-
Under the blanket of success,
Your body will dwell through the sensation-
Of revelation's proclamation of procreation

Think wet you get wet
Think debt you get debt
In what language is the manual of your mindset?
Don't fret what others say
It's your own thoughts that will pave your future
That's the truth of **The Secret**
And it's more tangible than splendid Kama sutra

ECHOES
OF VIOLENCE

As I Say

What's good for the Goose is good for the Gander
Kid grown up and can't seem to lift my standards
Live by the code of what I was handed
Love meant submitting to
Whatever his fist demanded
Buried the bruise on my spirit
It was so deeply branded
Looked up to the Heavens cause
I needed God to sand it down
And create it anew
Low self-esteem was spreading like the swine flu
Little girl mopping the floor
Backing up into a corner with my fears
Watched you let daddy beat you good
To the last drop of tears
Child-rearing left this tender soul
Without any protection
Then I looked up and you and daddy
Were back in deep affection
Then I looked down and momma was
On the ground turning different complexions
I don't like this bedtime story
Can someone change it's direction?

Poor momma thought I never did see it
Keenly naïve
Never thought I'd grow up to be it
I used to cover my eyes with the pillows
And with the sheets
Ears left open so through the cracks of the door
Domestic **V**iolence did seep
In a place of my own now
With abuse fixed like a painting on the wall
Daddy looked me in the eye and said
"Girl, aint you got no self-respect at all?"
Calling the kettle black was the pot
All the boxing matches in our home
He must've forgot
Yes, it's my story now and
I'm in the role of parent
Momma turned over in her grave and asked
Baby how did this happen?
Well momma, it should be apparent

Daddy said well if I did wrong
Then don't be like me
But I was already rooted from their example
Which was the first I did see

Now I'm wearing momma's shoes
And sharing beds with dad
My abusers were made in his image
No matter what face they had
Bad was the path I went down
Rape taught me to hold my tears in and
Not let my emotions make a sound
No closer friend than what lay in
My Cover Girl bag that was blue
Wiped the urine from my face
When they were all through

Someone once told me that women
Were to be loved and cherished, so I did expect it
But momma's reality told this little girl
"However a man treats you baby,
Just go on and accept it."

Do as I say not as I do
These are the words I heard from you
Do as I do not as I say
That's what your actions really conveyed

Do as I say not as I be
These are the words my daughter heard from me
Do as I say not as I be
This is how we planted and grew our family tree
From generational curses
May God set us all free

Do as I say not as I do
These are the words your children hear from you
Do as I do not as I say
PARENTS-
Today-
Choose to be a better display

Note: Mommy and Daddy, I forgive you as I pray you forgive your parents for anything they did or did not do that affected you. I believe you did the best you knew how as I do the best I know how as a parent now. I thank you for every good thing you've instilled in me and brought into my life and the lives of your grandchildren. I love you always.

Laura's Tears

Today I cried and it wasn't for myself
I traveled through the eyes of a woman
And saw that someone had stolen her wealth
Not the wealth you're familiar with-
Able to shake or fold
In the corners of her eyes-
I saw that someone had removed her soul

A flood came rushing down her face,
Clear liquid we call tears
This was just the doormat of the hell-
That had been her visitor for many years
Frightened like a newborn babe-
Taken from the comfort of the womb
No longer did she feel its protection,
So her fears began to bloom
I searched for words that would hug her-
In a way she'd never known
Lord guide my tongue in this moment-
For its next move could cause her to roam

Today I cried and it wasn't for myself
I tried on a woman's shoes and
Devastation was heartfelt
She assigned her mind to go back in time
And determine if her confusion-
Was just an illusion or someone else's intrusion
Life's a bitch and then you marry one-
Was her conclusion

Bad things happen to really good people
Everybody's walk through life-
Was not created equal
This time she has to experience change,
Not another sequel
Oh Lord speak!
So she knows you too have not deserted
She had a part in this
Yes, we have concerted

But I can do ALL things through Christ
And am forgiven of sins
Yes, it's in your Word
And right now her healing needs provoking
Assurance that she was not just pain's token
Her wounds have stood up and spoken
Domestic **V**iolence happens to way too many folks
And I cry out today for every woman-
Whose had abuse as her yolk

Today I cried and it wasn't for myself
I symbolically took a woman by the hand
And let her know that she could-
Take the bad literature off her mental shelf
In order stop the violence;
I had to stop the silence and
Let her know that she could be safe-
Never again to walk on eggs shells,
Being his bate
Afraid to rest her eyes at night-
Because she wouldn't know her fate
Trust in the Lord and
Take away your "perp's" power to negate

You've been in school before but-
Now there's a new teacher
New Life and happiness are-
The lesson's main feature
Have faith in one who is higher
And he'll make you a new creature

Then you and I can both stop crying-
As we watch each other live;
Instead of watch each other dying

Mourn and move from the past
No matter who is at fault-
Self-shame and self-blame-
Continue the assault
God's got a new spirit for you-
In His special vault
So halt and listen
You are not to broken to be fixed and
God says come unto me and rest

I'm not like man whose intentions have a disguise
You no longer have to be burdened
You can trade your baggage for a prize
Now just borrow God's vision in the mirror-
Because it uses different eyes
He still deems you phenomenal
And says from this too you shall rise

Today I cry cause I've been where you are;
Knowing firsthand how it feels to think-
That help is too far
I tell you as sure as I did it that-
YOU CAN WALK AWAY
If you can't see your own self-worth-
Then use your kid's future to run the freedom relay

Oh I cry cause I know how it feels-
To think you're stuck
But on the other side, there is a life-
That from his fist or bullets-
You don't have to duck

Today I cry cause like Dr. King-
I have a dream too;
That one day little boys and girls-
Can play Power Rangers or Ms. Pac Man;
Instead of having to watch-
Mom get her face bashed in and
Not know what to do

Today I cry cause I've been that woman
And that little girl
But by the grace of God-
I GOT OUT
Now let's fight this thing together
And help heal this world

Victim's Impact Statement

. . . Everyday when I bathe myself I am forced to look at my wounds and cry as I am reminded of how I got them. For the rest of my life I will experience this. I also am reminded of my attack when I look for clothes to wear from day to day and have to be mindful to wear something that doesn't show my ugly scars; so that I don't have to be troubled with stares and questions. For the rest of my life I will experience that.

Psalms 35:12-14 says "If an enemy were insulting me, I could endure it; if a foe were raising himself against me, I could hide from him. But it is you, a man like myself, my companion, my close friend, with whom I once enjoyed sweet fellowship" one of the reasons why dealing with my attack has been so hard is because of who did it. I was not physically accosted by a stranger on the street! I was not caught up in a drive by intended for another! I was not the victim of a bank robbery! I was attacked by my former fiancé! . . . someone who professed to love me, someone I confided in, someone I planned a future with, and someone I thought would protect me from danger; not be my danger! . . .

Resurrection

Kitchen floor, in a pool of my own blood, I was lying
As a man repeatedly stabbed me,
I could see that I was dying
And no one was around to hear me crying;
Except for the one who hears the faintest plea-
I called Jesus who I knew could deliver me
At that moment I positioned my faith-
So my life could get an extension too
You are looking at the Mona Lisa of-
What God will do

I had stabs in my back and stabs in my arms
Devil looked on with pride
As his advocates did me harm
Stabs in my stomach and stabs in my legs
No begging for my life as God was already ahead
One more stab, now in the neck
Devil high fived his peeps cause
My life he thought he wrecked
He must've forgot that Jesus died on the cross-
To set up my resurrect
And in that very moment it began to take affect
After that battle I had emotional and physical scars
The devil thought he destroyed me,
But he just raised the bar
Soon and very soon all will know-
The reason I was created
Success is belated but it's on time
Cause its God-dated

After that battle I had **22** stabs
The devil thought my destiny was up for grabs
Malcolm said it best devil-
You've been bamboozled, hoodwinked,
Had and led astray
God decreed my tomorrow,
So you can't rob me of today
You lost the battle before you even got started
This thing between me and Jesus
Cannot be departed
You lost because you brought a boy and
I came back with "The Man"
Jesus sho nuf had backup and a plan
He brought the Angels who are always down to ride
They said "Look here devil,
You can torture her, but-
SHE WILL NOT DIE"!
That was my resurrection
Now I want you to take a moment of-
Recollection of His reflection and
The devil's perplexion;
Every time Jesus provides you with protection
I say this with affection
Jesus died on the cross so you could-
Salvage your life's pieces under-
His love's protection and-
Not be restrained by sin's subjection

New breath in my body came down from Heaven
I'm not the same little girl,
But a woman with new leaven
I AM STILL because HE IS REAL!

He's the beginning and the end-
No need to pretend
Forget what you heard-
God has the last word
Lover of my soul, dressed me in confidence,
So now I stand bold-
Never again to be sold
He's the one who suffered and
The one who died
For all the stupid things I did and
Then tried to hide
He's my doctor, lawyer,
Father mother, sister, brother;
Like no other, my whole life He covers
He is my beauty never to age
He is why I keep coming to the stage
I'm America's Next Top Model of Victory
If you want to know if He can really save you-
Just take a look at me

To recite a cute little poem I did not come
Like Neo in The Matrix, I am the one;
To make a difference in this world that's major-
Using the gifts given to me by the Savior

There is nothing beyond my reach
I came from the one who created when He'd speak
Here's a revelation for me and for you
We're made from the same fabric as Him,
So the same things we can do
For each one of you God has a resurrection
Tell the devil It's OVER!
Let God take control and give you new direction

BROWN
SKINOLOGY

A Celebration of US

Welcome to a celebration of US
Welcome to a journey that is a-
Historical Reimbursement
Welcome to an artistic feast of gratitude-
For our ancestors and elders who paved the way
Welcome to putting down hatred and
Picking up love for one another
Welcome to putting our differences behind us
And saying I got your back my Sista or my Brotha
Welcome to telling Dr. Martin Luther King-
That we're dreaming too
Welcome to telling Rosa Parks thanks-
For not giving up her seat
Otherwise things would be very different-
For me and for you
Welcome to giving it up to-
Our dear Sista Madame CJ Walker-
For creating the straightening comb,
That works magic on our hair

Welcome to humbling ourselves-
Before the memory of those;
Who for our benefit-
Were beaten on their backs that were bare
Welcome to saluting Mae Jamison who said-
I can travel to places that are beyond this earth
Welcome to honoring those whose actions said-
Black people, Know-Your-Worth!
Welcome to sharing the courage of those like
Kunte Kinte-
Who said you will not change my name
Welcome to smiling proudly for Shirley Chilsom
Who said-
I'm going to get up in politics and
Help change the game
Welcome to thinking of Frederick Douglass-
Every time you pick up a book
Welcome to thanking Professor Carte G. Woodson-
Who helped create a month;
Wherein, not our downfalls,
But at our accomplishments,
People would look

Welcome to praising our ancestor mothers
From the scraps of Massa's table,
They put together a feast so others they could feed
Welcome to humbling ourselves before the memory
Of those who for the freedoms we enjoy today,
Did indeed bleed
Welcome to lifting up the memory of Harriet Tubman
Her actions said,
If you think we gone stay in these chains-
Somebody done told you a lie
She helped many slaves escape,
Always stayed strapped
And taught us the real meaning of "ride or die"
Welcome to envisioning our ancestors-
On slave ships-
Sleeping in their vomit and feces
When asked "Why don't you just give up nigga?"
They look far into the future and said-
Because of He and She
See, they saw way beyond what was just in front
They got high off wanting a better life-
Not just some blunt
Welcome to loving and respecting ourselves-
Getting **Domestic Violence** out of our homes
Welcome to showing our ancestors-
They did not struggle in vain-
Cause we carry their bones
Welcome to the ride

US 101

Being a parent is living an example-
Not some cute "baby be real" stage
When my daughter cries, it's not recorded
God sent her to help me get my life in order
She is a self check and her life-
I am to direct, not wreck
So, my associates must have a spiritual reflect;
As I can expect her to do as I do more than as I say
Reality assigns me to do some God mirroring;
If I want her to go the right way

Bitch, slut, hoe, skank, tramp, or trick-
We've all heard this-
Even if just part of a play or skit
Nigga, punk bitch, mutha fucka,
Or original playa from the Himalayas
These are the names we were called yesterday-
But what will our names be tomorrow?
The same ole same if a new mind set isn't Purchased
Instead of borrowed

We devote too much quality time to-
Judging others for their mistakes
The plan of the Father is for us to-
Help one another's lives get reshaped

Sistas, if a brotha hurt you, dig up forgiveness
I aint fronting like that's easy-
I just know that's Kingdom business

Brothas, if you've been dogging these women-
Ask God to help you be a righteous man
Messing over your Sistas-
Just puts slavery back in command

God created the world in 7 days and
There is no work greater
He took Adam's rib to make Eve-
Knowing men would need someone-
To have their backs later
Revolutions don't happen with just one sex alone
Together they create the right balance and
Set things in the forward zone
Some real love for one another we need to find
Hating on each other is a design for the blind
As is my goal, I pray I've said at least one thing-
That made a difference
Let's keep each other lifted
Class is dismissed
Thanks for listening

Re-born

What are we doing?
Self denial is just self screwing
Looking in the mirror and not sure who it is we see
Cause we're living in reverse
From the past we've not been freed
Today I spit to plant a seed,
For the often hushed need-
For a woman to say-
"Everything can't be his fault!"
Some of the blame is mine
I allowed him to be the waster of my time;
Fucking me from behind and keeping me behind
Some of yall looking at me crazy but whatever
Cause I'm tired of the blind leading the blind
There are some real hidden truths-
In that button called rewind
If you get off your need to be the victim-
Maybe some peace you can find

I don't excuse these fools for their actions
I'm just trying to move into a life-
That's positively impacted
So I have to do the math and maturely accept-
The part of the madness that was my fraction
Right now I'm having contractions and
The new woman in me is coming forth into this life-
With a new attitude and she'll get different reactions

If you could swallow something other than cum-
LONG enough to listen;
Maybe on your own heart,
You could stop the pissing
Don't get stuck on my graphic Ebonics and miss this
You actually need to get close enough to kiss this

You aint got to ride as nobody's trick but-
Rule with your trade
Just like in the game of chess;
Multitasking greatness is how the Queen was made
Not your vagina
But your character is the real grenade
For the riches in it, no higher price could be paid-
Than the true sacrifice of the life that Jesus laid
Turn God's frown upside down
Grab hold of the common sense He gave you
And get back on solid ground

Brothas, stop saying all women are crazy
They just got messed up from your shit
And it made their senses hazy
Don't trip-
You aint got to bail
I'm not here to start Part II of-
Waiting to Catch Hell
You, I'm not here to scold
US, I just want to remold
You, I don't hate-
I just seek to mate with your reasoning cause-
Some things you did to me personally,
Took some ingredients out my seasoning
Now during arguments, the more I listen;
I see the product of at least 2 generations-
Of men and women,
That were never reconditioned
So Black Men and Black Women-
Can we finally get this thing right?
So that the little boys and girls-
Coming up behind US-
Can behold a future without fright-
Of becoming the very thing that either-
We've seen or we've been;
Which is just another form of slavery all over again

Tonight I put down flares in this poetry venue-
Because relationships between Our men & women-
Have become features of the walking dead menu-
Send you this sermon;
Allowing God to use me-
While delivering the learning
Known and unknown my love for you is real
Have to release these truths from the lion's den;
No longer can conceal
It's time to start the revolutionary orgy, strip down,
And let the truth be revealed-
So we all can really heal
Our troubled souls need to be refined
Material and physical showcases are human nature
But display your beautiful mind

Black people-
We are a sought after race
But we have to stop settling for just being-
A way to ensure someone's son or daughter-
Has a pretty face
Our values have been misplaced
We don't see our own greatness-
Or the beauty of one another
Drop us on a blank page and
There you will find the knowledge that is power,
Not just some color
I'm so tired of us spending our money on bullshit;
Often known as a race that gets "blinged" up and
Decked out in furs and feathers
While other races save their money and
Open businesses together
We be chilling on the couch, watching TV and
Grubbing on pork hot-dogs
You better get you a plan B, C, and D-
Cause aint no guarantees in a job

Sorry if this seems abrupt
But somewhere along this journey;
US supposed to be freed negroes-
Got life fucked up
You have to be good for more than "nuttin"-
If you want in the future,
Your family to have somethin
Oh we are the great entertainers
We can rap, dance, and sing
But it's time to take the masks off the real "massa"
And stop asking-
"Why won't my freedom ring?"
God did not create a nation of slaves;
Mapped out a plan to give us free
We all have divine assignments to complete,
While we're down here
And He's up there preparing our homes
WAAAAAKKKKEEEE UUUUUUUUUUUUPPPPPPPPPP!
And get in your destiny's zone

I'm calling all my brothas to stop-
Lying down with anything
And start standing up for greater things-
That can take you higher like angel's wings
I'm calling all my sistas to stop hating on each other
And start loving and supporting each other-
Then cover these brothas when they get stupid
And revert back to sin
Holding each other up is the only way;
We as a people are gonna win
My poet's journey parallels the truth
And sometimes can be morbid
I give this message to the messengers-
So some "real talk" can go forward
We've allowed twisted mentality-
To become our storage
We take in all this trash but
Want someone else to pay for storage

Where's my Huey Newton, Dr. King,
Gil Scott Heron, and Marcus Garvey?
Brothas, you gotta be more than just-
That nigga who can start the party
Where's my Rosa Parks, Harriet Tubman,
And Angela Davis?
Sistas, our crowns are falling off,
But if we dig up our roots-
We can repave this
I seek more than snaps and claps-
When I put down this art form
God sent me to set it off-
Cause it's time to be reborn

Just US

What is justice?
Is it just US fending for our damn selves?
Just US still being beaten with the sticks of hatred
Or burned with the water-
From hoses of unacceptance?
What is justice?
It is said to be in union with morals and ethics;
Yet even with a lack of evidence-
A man's pleas for the truth to come forth-
Still gets rejected
What is justice?
Is it not satisfactory that he already sacrificed
20 years of his free?
Not good enough that over 900,000 strong joined-
Hearts and for him cried out on their knees?
Including those negroes who made it-
Inside "the big house"
And are seemingly accepted by society
But peep the depth of the situation and you'll find;
That underneath they are still-
Seen as the nigger prodigy
Oh great God in me . . . I dare not question your ways
Fight hard to never disrobe self of its mustard seed;
As we deal with Just US Days
What is justice?
In the words of a great King
"Free at last! Free at last!
Thank God almighty-
We are free at last!"
Yet not able to get past a wrongful execution
This revolution was televised but-

The family of officer Mark MacPhail-
Felt a sense of relief;
While the family of Troy Davis bathed in their whys
Trials were made to be fair with man being-
Innocent until proven guilty;
But September 21st showed us that innocent-
Is a verdict that gets changed to guilty
When people get drunk off their authority
System sorority sworn to act according to
What they personally feel
Fuck your appeal!
Of evidence that is way more tricky
than a glove that didn't fit
It was absent from the courthouse and
echoed "not present" from the jail cell;
of a man who failed by being-
in the wrong place at the wrong time
Dime dropped on him but
who actually did the crime?
True grit and grime reeks from the scales of
lady liberty
A white woman can drown her child and walk;
but the innocent Black man-
cannot be heard when he talks . . . NO!
Because every now and then one of "them";
might have to take one for the team
and be made an example
But Just US get put up on the block-
like a DJ spinning samples

Can't go to sleep tonight;
cause I'm a mother whose son could've been-
at Burger King in Georgia that night
If you think slavery is ova;
I've got some contrary news fo ya
What is Justice?
Or better yet
What is Justice for ALL?
There was no sign of it-
the night Troy Davis got the death call
Fall-ing down yet religiously trying to get up
He went to his grave hanging on to hope real tough
You'd think if he went to the courthouse-
instead of the whorehouse;
then he wouldn't end up fucked
Stuck on the racism that subscribes to;
the mentality of "Cover Girl"
Serpents in sheep's clothing
Welcome to the real Real World
What is Justice?
Just Us fending for our damn selves
Just Identification of **C**ourthouse **E**xtortion
Just Innocent **C**onvicts **E**xecuted
Just Investing in protests hoping to **C**reate **E**xtensions
Just Ignoring lack of **C**rucial **E**vidence
Just Icing on the **C**ake of **E**xcruciating reality
Justice
Just US

The Races of Racists

I'm not racist
I don't hate races-
Because I've come to the end of-
Too many races only to have someone-
Of identical skin;
With feet stretched out to make sure I don't win
Sin is sin
I've had some unthinkable things done to me-
By even my own kin
So I deal with the spirit of a man cause-
They may call the white man "massa" but-
Would my brotha or my sista hurt me-
If opportunity said they can?

Stand above that parallel thinking
We sinking cause you won't move past the past
Yeah, I know white people used to tear into dat ass;
One way or another but-
When you're not walking the kingdom mile anyway-
Who's to blame brotha?
Wearing rubbers of hatred-
To protect you from being more
Our ancestors need you to carry the torch,
Not even the score-
Cause there's more

I don't deny that your anger is justified
But if that's all we're made of-
Then, how will we rise?
Cause hatred is a disease and hatred is a chain . . .
Same as the ones-
Slaves were locked in
But the mind has the option to be free;
If you take their mistake and turn the key
See, I can't watch a lil white girl-
Get beaten and raped and be satisfied;
All because my "people" rode the same ride
Alive are my morals sent from God
You the same "massa" you claim to hate-
If a new path you don't trod
Why do you really hate white people anyway?
We (Black people) were the ones who taught-
"How to Be a Slave Owner" back in the day

Is it better because at least we enslaved we?
It's all the same genocide if you rob-
Another human being of their free
Be the reason this shit stops not-
The DJ who plays this tragedy on repeat
Be a positive successor and
Someone worth writing about-
Then you will have delivered true defeat
Seat on the throne can take it from here
We create a legacy of injustice by living in the rear

Not telling you to forget any of their licks,
Broken skin from cracked whips and
Young women groomed into whores
Just need your intellect to soar cause-
There's more to the race-
Than races and we can't win the race-
By raising new racists

Understand the reality of an enemy but-
Be careful not to share his mirror
"Strange Fruit" will always bring jolts of pain
But in this moment I see much clearer,
What it is I am to be-
According to the job description in Heaven
It's time to love ourselves then each other and
Constantly break new leaven-
Of knowledge
Just share what your experiences taught you;
If your finances didn't provide the luxury of college . . .
It's cool cause everyday life is a school-
So make sure your learning the lessons
Cause you never know whose problem-
You might be assigned to address and
Even confess your failed tries;
Understanding that this could be the reason-
That person lives instead of dies

Black Man

You are not my accident
You are my accent
You are not my mistake
You are my mystery
You are not my sin
You're my healing within
You are not my fuck up
You're my fervor for the future
You are not a Massa's nigger
You're God's footsteps
Onto paths that are much bigger
You are that Black Man

You're the rock I can rely on
The cemetery my problems die on
So faithful to me, no need to spy on
So real with me, no one could ever lie on
The inspiration from which I wrote this poem on
You are that Black Man

Some people question how we even came to be but
You are so much more-
Than the white of their eyes can see
You are the opposite and balance-
That I constantly seek
You possess a charm that causes my inner bitch-
To shift down to meek . . .
Without making me feel weak
You are that Black Man

More amazing than any other being
Through hard times pray over me
True manhood decreeing
From the fears of my past,
Your love has got me fleeing
Sipping on your encouragement in me-
Yes, now I'm believing
You are that Black Man

You take care of the kids
So I can have some time to myself
You even sit me down to-
Discuss the stats of my health
I asked God for a companion but with you-
He superseded my wealth
You are that Black Man

You wash the clothes, fix the toilet,
And change my tires
So sexy in your apron cooking up whatever I desire
Handling your business 9 to 9 style
Always reserve some energy-
So we can get buck wild
I massage your everything and
You do yoga techniques with my legs
Stares exchanged soul to soul-
Nothing left to be said;
As our minds and bodies are fed
In all that you do it is done well
You secure me like no other-
No more Waiting to Exhale
Cause **You are that Black Man**

You peep me on game,
So I can survive in these streets
Got me reading your books,
So the same language we'll speak
Kingdom wardrobe wrapped around your mind
Revolutionary breed-
You'll change the whole world in time
One can search many races but will never find
Beautiful Black Man you are one of a kind

If what I feel for you isn't right, I'll accept the wrong-
For however long our journey on this earth lasts
You more than make up for all the-
Sorry "lil boys" who hurt me in the past
You are that Black Man

You're that my part of my life that seems surreal
Your friendship defrosts me so now I can feel
You poured liquid affirmations-
Into my dehydrated heart
Your visions motivate me to do more than my part

You're a blessing that's undressing
River of serenity remove all my stressing
The way I have your back will never be lessening
You showed my what you're working with;
So my spirit stopped wrestling
Our bond is so profound,
Got scholars second guessing
Fate performed our ceremony,
No need in haters protesting
I wash and love your dirty "draws" yes,
I'm confessing
Cause **You are that Black Man**

IN SYNC

The Wrong One

Mama never told me that candy bars had legs
He was a picture of perfection;
 whether you started at his feet or the top of his head
Firm believer of business and pleasure are-
2 things that should never mix
But with all the emotional hell I was going through,
 he could be a great "fix"
He had electricity in the corners of his smile
I knew from the 1st moment I saw him,
I'd need to avoid him for a while
I took the extra long way to my office
and made sure his bus I'd never ride
He was so SEXY!
Only by staying away could the denial-
of my curiosity survive
Almost a year later and
I was still trying to hold my ground
Then a co-worker told me he left for another job
and the answer to the prayer I should've prayed,
I thankfully found

Early 1 morning, while sitting at the bus station;
a sweet aroma hit me with just the right sensation
It smelled like a candle filled with
Marc Jacobs cologne
I looked up to check its entrance and there he was-
6 ft 6 chocolate fantasy coming through my zone
Turns out he had 1 more day to work-
before he officially left
and the slick way he approached me,
took on a permanent affect
While dropping passengers off,
he caught a glimpse of me
and began to head in my direction
To my surprise I experienced an internal erection
He offered his hand like Billie D Williams-
In Lady Sings the Blues
I didn't want his arm to fall off-
so embracing his big strong hands-
was the path that I decided to choose
He spoke to me in a way that was-
previously unknown
Every syllable was gentle and carried deep tones
I asked him if he would get in trouble-
for leaving his passengers on the bus
He said he didn't care because this might be-
his last chance to see if there could be an us
At that moment my heart hit the floor
My body felt immovable-
as I gave him a look that said;
oh you can shoot and score
After a brief conversation,
he made sure I had more than 3 ways to reach him
and like Gregory Hines watched Gloria in
Waiting to Exhale;
I watched him walk away with anticipation-
that was leaking

He turned around midway to his bus and
offered a magical salutation
I knew if he ever got me alone,
the night would be longer than-
a law student's dissertation

An older gentleman tapped me on my shoulder
He said mercy, that young man's got smooth-
written all over his folder
Instantly I came to know the true meaning
of Captain Hook
Cause once he reeled me in-
I couldn't leave even if I was shook
Long conversations took up all my time
Every thought was stolen by him
I think I was going blind

He called to say Good Morning Beautiful
and Goodnight my Angel
The way he made me feel outweighed-
the brilliance of the star spangled
He was my beast and I was his beauty
I was trying to be good but I wasn't sure-
how much longer I could hold on to the booty
Soon we consecrated our unidentified status-
at a place that had many rooms
Surely if I frequent this place enough,
there'd be matrimony in bloom
He said I needed a man to pay my bills
and take care of me in every way
Plus he put it on me so tough;
It didn't matter if he broke every promise-
the very next day
Eventually I began to wear the pants
and still opted to stay

I was truly caught up in an emotional tangle
I couldn't possibly find anyone better than him-
so my insecurities wore his words like-
some brand new bangles
With him I felt a fiery passion;
like that of Pocahontas and John Adams
Good or bad, being with another man-
was something I could not fathom
We gave each other pet names
Now how cute is that
I probably could've seen clearer if the view-
wasn't taken on my back
His nickname was Romeo and mine was Juliet
I even called him that in public-
If his ego needed a pet

Fairy tales are known for their happy endings-
so you might not like the end of this
I finally landed on my stomach and knew
I had to get out of this shit!
I stuck my head out of the castle
but I was not looking for him
I looked up to the heavens and
knew it was time for my knees to bend
This relationship kept me hitting a brick wall
I had gone back in time to when-
Adam and Eve created man's great fall
My heart asked God for answers as I began to cry
I clearly heard His voice say-
"I forgive you, but, to you,
Romeo must die!"
Ladies, don't SETTLE for ROMEO
WAIT for your KING

Something New

Lover,
You awake me as you shake me-
By the gentle biting of my breasts,
Leaking with honey sapped milk
Rubbing my thighs that are softer than silk
Later my backside obediently tilts and
Toes bend within my stilts
Lights, Camera, Action Captain-
Capture every fraction of this erotic interaction
Like a skilled ballerina I stretch and moan
We're not engaged in child's play,
We're both sexy and grown
I'm dreaming of the entrance of your shaft-
That's about a foot long
Do Me Baby by Prince is the appropriate song-
For this all night long
Allow all 12+6 inches to set sail-
Around my vocal cavity,
Without any force,
Just the pleasures of natural gravity
Had to be amazing when you hoisted me in mid air-
Like a car on blocks;
Waiting to be worked and
As you repeatedly entered I jerked with a smirk-
Because I too felt amazed when I discovered-
A whole new world
Praying more orgasms prevail and
With faith in you I prepared my wails
Oh how I love to learn and
You are a passionate teacher
Hang-gliding between my 2nd lips and
Devouring the river that had seeped her . . .

Tongue stood strong thru quivers-
To show her gratitude . . .
Only to be overthrown by background chatter
Gave notice to the fact that-
Other parts of my vehicle needed service too
But you gazed me into assurance that-
After 2 ½ hours of labor,
You weren't hardly thru and
Actually had plans to show me-
Something New

Not Easy

Things were easy when we were just fucking
and feelings were tucked in
Then just my luck, in love I fell
My insides do aerobics to the very thought of you-
Is how I can tell
So immaculately amazing;
you could probably sell it to anyone
Your arms are my hiding place
Your strong man hands spank me
and I pick up the pace
Your eyes remind me of God's grace
Your voice that shares your past struggles;
reflect God's face that I draw on my-
mental etch-a-sketch and
it comes out looking like a rainbow
I am the president of your fan club
The head cheerleader of your team
The beat of your drum
The Trinity to your Neo
The preacher of your message
and whatever your soul needs-
I want to address it
But we're just having fun right
Night after night, turned week after week
Every day we have to speak and
plan our next retreat and
I'm getting the best damn sleep of my life!
But we wade in a sea of uncomfortable strife
We're treading upon waters that are thin
Feels sooooooo good it must be a sin
Oh will God just allow me some forgiveness on lend
I said I DO once and it was painful-
so I can't do it again

See things were easy when we were just fucking
and feelings were tucked in
Then just your luck, in love you fell

Aw look at this
Now you all on my shit
Talking about "How'd she get a nigga like this?"
See I'm a hit it and run nigga;
but on my heart she pulled a trigger
Got me spitting about matrimony and having a kid
Yeah, that hard ass nigga is pissed-
cause he thought he was just playing another chick-
but the hustler in him got dismissed and replaced-
by the man who craves loves passion like a child
and the man who was conquered-
by the bliss of a kiss,
that says "I love yo Black ass!"
and that aint no shit cause I can't make it pass

We're in too deep and want to keep-
the "IT" we've grown accustomed too
and I'm so cool with calling you my Boo
but I just can't repeat the words I DO
My heart is still mending so I can't be a fool x 2

Things were easy when we were just fucking
and feelings were tucked in
Now just our luck in love we fell
Physical ties are a dangerous spell

It was sooooooo easy when we were just fucking
And feelings were tucked in

BUT
Some things in life do not reside on Easy Street
And we're
Not Easy

False Equation

I equated our sex with love-
because that's what I needed it to be
I equated our sex with love-
because emotionally I was not free
I equated our sex with love-
for the same reasons many women do
I equated our sex with love-
for a wholeness that could not be found in you
I equated our sex with love-
like wishing upon a star
I equated our sex with love-
even when the presence of orgasm was too far
I equated our sex with love-
because I hadn't yet experienced it with myself
I equated our sex with love-
because I had misplaced, for me, God's wealth
I equated our sex with love-
because I needed someone to listen
I equated our sex with love
as the down stroke and my pain started reminiscing

I equated our sex with love-
because I sought payment for all my duties
I equated our sex with love-
to close the blinds that showed,
you would just use me
I equated our sex with love-
as I felt my time clock start to ticking
I equated our sex with love-
as I tired of my own wound licking
I equated our sex with love-
so I could participate in conversations too
I equated our sex with love-
because the mending of my heart wasn't through
I equated our sex with love-
like a prostitute who prays she will not burn
I equated our sex with love-
because my map faded for my own concerns
I equated our sex with love-
because I needed to so bad

I equated our sex with LOVE-
That thing
I
Never
Had

**This poem is dedicated to every Miss Ceely
And Precious of the world.**

Is this what love has become?

Just some misplaced feelings on the run
A dick with a get out of jail free card-
searching for some fun
A broken heart that couldn't see the truth-
if it was as bright as the sun

Is this what love has become?

Love is supposed to make our freedom ring;
so why on the flip side does it create-
the most painful thing,
changing all the songs we sing

Is this what love has become?

A game of me using you
and you trying to see if you can use me faster
WE trying to be crowned master of-
"I won't be hurt anymore"
Others look on to see which one of us-
will be standing last;
because their love has begun to bore
It's a crying shame we fight to monitor-
how far cupid comes within our "space"
Truth is, sometimes love can be an ugly place

Is this what love has become?

Mama told me that love was special and pure;
so how come every time I breathe it-
I feel so unsure and insecure;
wondering if another round of it, I can endure
and if I suffer one more knock out-
will God even be enough to cure

Is this what love has become?

Daddy said baby,
there are other fish in life's big ocean
But I'm starting to think-
that is just a band aid notion;
cause a past fish still has me
hooked on his potion
and I'm motioning for relief

My brother said why you mad?
That nigga wasn't shit!
I don't understand why you hurting like this

It hurt cause I wasted years of my life-
on that long ass trip
and now I'm here having to sip on
"What in the hell just happened?"

My girlz said fuck him!
Just get a new captain
So here I am setting sail again
Cause that's the way love goes

What Does It Mean

What do people mean when they say-
"I Love You"?
I want to experience love
I want to make love as opposed to just having sex-
with someone who's merely
present to fuck me . . . over
Tired of sharing my depth while crying
on fake shoulders
Now older and feel how much colder
the world really is
Don't want to invest in one who is no better than-
less the feces of a dead dog . . .
fog clearing from my windows;
bright view of my sins-
though I still want and deserve to experience love-
of one who is not just here when it's cool-
or if I can provide free rent while he-
school's me with hard ass lessons
I want a man who thinks my fat is-
PHAT (Pretty Hot and Tempting)-
carefully listening
and strokes my ego thru its venting but-
ever unrelenting with the honesty of a true friend
Lends me his shirt to wipe my tears
with bless-ed assurance-
that his love won't make things disappear;
like the commitment and acts of faith that-
get moved to the rear by many who take-
their eyes for a walk in bad times cause-
there are good and plenty of-
others out there and
they don't have to go thru this shit

Yeah they can just get with the next chick-
or dick and not have to say-
"Aint this about a B.I.T.C.H."!
Bogus **I**nterpretations **T**hat **C**astrate **H**omes
Is "I Love You" just 3 words that roam-
or sound cute in a poem?
Where art thou whom wilt love me-
in a manner without conditions?
Free to really be me

Dancing with me to Natalie Cole's
Inseparable . . . yes we are
Like a flower to a tree, like words to a melody
Or as I brown sugar it
Like the perfect verse over a tight beat and
I love you beyond your big feet . . .
so treat yourself to a full course of-
some of this here soul food cause;
just one helping would be cruel to your true desires
Black man I hold the unchanging hand of
He who sits up higher
Authored the love that has none greater . . .
so later we can embrace one another with the same
I need one who will pause thru storms and
call His name . . . before mine
That type of reverence will
stand the tests of the grind and
bind us with forever's ropes
Don't need pharmaceutical remedies to cope . . .
just each other-
tied together with the infinity of trinity

I want a man who loves himself enough
to not unlove me
Sees God's ways to resolve a situation-
instead of 1-2 combinations-
of ring side professionals
Not afraid to make confessionals
of how in the dark he cries;
about things in his past he cannot deny
Carries a permanent marker,
writing letters of apology-
to the other Women he hurt or
children he never cared for,
just gave a donation for birth
Worth forgiveness is his sincere remorse and
vows to change his course;
knowing that this is the beginning of his healing too
Trials of my past and things I did or had done
that I wish I could put some white-out thru
So let's jump the broom as a symbol of defeating all-
who would put us asunder . . .
no wonder how we're going to survive cause-
mercy did the intro and grace gave us high fives
OH what do people mean when they say-
"I Love You"?
Well I cannot outline your dictionary
But on my terms;
for me to abandon my man-
I'd have to be buried

Dear Love,

I have waited for you in blocks that can't be timed and numbers that can't be calculated. I've cried over the presence of your imposters till my cup runneth over and the deserts were no longer dry. Try-ing to swim through the ducts as a means of escape from the pain felt when confusion and I closed the door behind those I thought were you leaving. I had irregular breathing with a heart that was no less than twice broken; mere token for your stroking. Stumbling through repeated journeys got me choking as I've cum to realize many evenings I've met have not the beauty of a multicolored sunset, which holds no regrets as it is going down. Unlike those of us who search in the dark with no light because we've gone blind and more invitations are accepted without review. Stopped operating under that which walks not by sight. Oh Love! I plead you cause I need you to understand what it means to be complete. Take a seat by your feet. Counseled by whole numbers but a hole in 1 makes room for the place of a stake that is too high. Creates a cadence of whys from not finding the Mr. who signs his checks with the last name Right.

Hoping to be yours truly,
D

Wish List

I wish I knew
How it felt to have someone cleanse the juice-
From my honey dew
To the stories of others' heated encounters,
I've listened
Realizing that I'm so out of touch with this subject
I can't even reminisce
For I've never made love and
Can't recall my last kiss

I wish I knew
How it felt to have trouble doing normal things-
Like straight walking
All because of an energetic lover-
Who kept my lips talking;
With no gaps in the conversation
Hypnotic relations
With a patience for positions that could puzzle me
Unlike imposters of lovers who heard my desires
And took it as a sign to merely muzzle me

I wish I knew
How it felt to be bitten deep
Trio of lips, tip of the tongue, and teeth
Uniquely skilled with the assurance-
Of a dedicated freak
Random permission slips for my truth to leak
And unveil a reflection of my insides erections
Polishing a golden apple for their instructor
Conductor, who allowed a little girl . . .
The promotion to a woman

I wish I knew
Of a lover who would come home to me
And massage away my day until I was free
From all of it's careless whispers
Then joyfully rub me thoroughly with organic oils
As he believes in the healing power-
Of untainted things
And only the absolute best
To me, he wanted to bring

I wish I knew
Of the intrusion of a break-in to my back side
By one who'd ride me till the sun's rise
Then wipe my tears as they fall
Call-in all things creepin to hurt me-
To exit our room's walls;
Because he would provide all the security-
I'll ever need . . .
Making me want to find our program's button
And hit high speed or fast play-
So we could do it again without delay

OH I wish I knew
Of a man who would allow my manicured toes-
To reside . . .
In his mouth's confide;
While synchronizing strokes to my front side
Using the gutter words of role play
Ensuring no part of me is left behind
And behind is where he would release his journey
He put in so much work
I might need to switch my bed for a gurney
But it's all good

I wish I knew
Of a real man who understood that these wishes-
Cannot come true by just anyone
Requirements of one who sees fit to
Ask my Father in Heaven for my hand;
Taking commands from him first
I know I have yearnings but
For any "Joe" they do not thirst
Lessons of former mistakes
I pray they were the worst
Now I wish upon the one beyond the stars
For the lover who will join with me
In the embracing a second creation

Love Me Like

Love me like everything "Old School"
Love me like the absence of rules
Love me like your-
"I really need to throw these away
but them my favorite shoes"
Love me like your mama's-
"That's my good shit!" jewels
Love me like without conditions-
just as our a Heavenly Father
Love me like your favorite song on the radio
Love me like you want everyone inhaling to know
Love me like a kid on the swings at the park
Love me like what we do-
don't have to be done in the dark
Love me like your favorite DVD
Love me like being with someone else-
Is something you cannot see
Love me like Southern Beignets with,
warm chocolate sauce-
from the Grand Lux
Love me like you can't wait to-
one day marry me in a tux
Love me like a day off from the job
Love me like the little girl within me-
no longer has to sob
Love me like the very air you breathe
Love me like that priceless gift-
you weren't expecting to receive

Love me like TGIF (Thank God it's Friday)
and I just got paid
Love me like the secret someone told you-
that helped you bypass an early grave
Love me like a child who no longer-
needs to leave on the night light
Love me with your everything
Love me like right

The Truth

Outside looking at the sky-
whose beauty resembles the truth in your eyes;
that changes the whys that tried to crush me
You occupied my side and told my falling tears-
they would be the last of their kind-
God's sign of a resurrection of the heart
One part of me dies yet another gets a fresh start
You are my new beginning and
if fate does not allow me to kiss the sun tomorrow-
just off our bond thus far-
I'd leave here winning

You and I

I possess a constant desire-
for the mental enhancement
and ever bonding friendship-
encountered when in your company
Majestic craving for a physical initiation of our love
When we wrap ourselves in the blanket of passion,
warmed with the heat of seduction
and later cooled by a satisfying retirement
As many reminisce on the glories of History-
so shall I dwell in our bedtime stories;
feeding off morsels of the sweet memories of-
You and I

One Man Band

You're so special to me;
I don't think you really understand
What you do for me as a Friend,
Lover and Teacher-
no one else can-
cause I won't let them
The auditions are over
I've made you my one man band and
I'll walk on burning sand for your happiness
Now when I have visions,
It's no longer I but we-
that I hold in my sight
Our souls have become parallel and
that's what makes this union alright
Your new membership on my team,
has become my sleeping pill at night
When you're out in this world and
people try to hinder you with shit
Know that from the depths of my-
heart and soul,
It's realness that I "spit"
When you're experiencing disappointment-
or hard times come your way
Reminisce on the treasures I bring
and know that with me-
It's a brand new day
I'm not here to hurt you;
just want to help you as you turn your life around

I'm filling out the papers so I can copyright-
how to turn your frown upside down
Luther Van Dross said Wait for Love
and you've been waiting for a while
Rest assured you've got the right one baby
and if ever you're in need-
my number should be on speed dial
You've changed the wardrobe of my spirit and
given me the enthusiasm of a child
If I were standing at the wishing well;
I'd only ask for you because-
you're the manufacturer of my smile
You're my Appetizer, my Dinner and my Dessert
I could go on and on-
professing the vastness of your worth
You are always there for me
and always there for the kids
If there were a city wide auction of REAL men;
on you, no one could even afford to bid
Outside or behind closed doors we be "wylin"
Doing the damn thing
Boy where did you get your stylin?
You are so good to me;
up to Heaven I start to dial and
Give a "shout out" to God-
because you are the capital M-A-N
I told God if He was looking for suggestions,
for a new creation-
He could just make yo ass all over again!

This Is What You Do

I can find another man out there this is true;
but with the riches of your heart there are only few-
intertwine with my soul and make it do what it do-
the morning loses all its good without you
It aint even really about sex;
that's just how you and I reconnect
We can fuck other people but
won't have the same effect
We're not even in control
creator made the connect
At the end of the day more time I wanna borrow;
cause when I'm in your presence
I see new tomorrows
Like Johnson & Johnson-
promise no more tears of sorrow
Your gentle seize of my fears is the best by far
OH your spankings make me giddy up-
like a race horse that's winning
Each and every day you're my new beginning
You elevate the woman in me
You are the one I hear my eyes plea
Unlike previous cats you want my vision to be good
and never blind
Got me smiling so hard-
stars asking how do I keep my shine
Our silent conversations have many exclamations
To be every woman for you is my forever declaration

OH I just had to let you know-
I'm so anxious to carry your seed;
I already got that pregnant woman's glow
Over and over you give me free and
like good music, you take me on rich journeys
You're my Olympian in and out of the sheets
You call me Brown Sugar and
you're my perfect verse over a tight beat
When I think of our situation
I swear I'm being punked;
cause even when you pray for me-
it sounds like spoken funk
Whatever I'd risk to be with you it would be worth it
Even your flaws are sexy
Boy you're damn near perfect
Valedictorian of your species-
even your walk has an alert and
I marked a national holiday on the calendar-
for the day that you were birthed
And God added an eighth day for your creation-
just to prove His love is true
Your conscious stamina holds me-
through all the shit that I go through
Before you, life was just another verse of-
BB King's *Down Home Blues*
There'll never be a better harvest-
than the love I reap from you

Can I

Building on friendship but
Is it okay to say you I love?
No other above you except-
The one from whence you came
And said tomorrow He'll change your whole frame
Not just another lame who hooked up with a dame
We're so much the same;
Feels like we're already sharing last names
And I'll take the blame for this bond
I know times mirror hard but
Look up and you'll see a pond;
Filled with fresh water, without conditions
Stop giving fear admission
Change the doubt channel
And listen to my heart-
That speaks nothing but the truth;
So pure it can give you back your youth
Not like the First Lady Eve,
Giving you death's fruit
But the over qualified candidate;
Looking to suit every need you recruit me to handle
No other has a longer burning candle,
For what it is you yearn
Front row student, eager to learn and
Discern through every situation
I know others have left wounds but
I can re-write your joy's emancipation
Creation of your very need to breathe
And conceive your God given goal

No more half steps-
Just whole
Command your soul to connect with mine
Check mate
When union is apparent,
He will set the date for fate
Throwing you some bait-
Will you bite it-
To become undivided?
Can't hide it
I ride it
Rumors can't get beside it
Sometimes I cry cause it hurts-
So good to love so much
Nothing moves me more except-
The Master's touch
We'll combine to make His-tory;
Filled with many stories
Fighting to live off Trust
May God get all the glory
As for me-
I take this union rich or poor
See, I be rooted from what's under the floor
Mine so genuine
Wide open
Serving you with all my feelings' dominion
So I'm asking . . .
Can I love you?

In Ways

You are what wonderful-
Wants to be when it grows up
When you enter a room, my happiness shows up
So unbelievable I pinch myself to see if it's authentic
So sinfully good-
I'm at the altar preparing for repentance
Checking the calendar to see if it's April Fool's Day-
But I saw that it wasn't so
Some reciprocity I want to send your way

I want to touch you and kiss you in ways-
That let you know with me, you'll never be hurt
In ways that have you
Walking around in the daytime-
With a flashlight just to do a search
In ways that let you know without a doubt-
For you, there's a Heaven on earth

I want to touch you and kiss you in ways-
That make time stand still
In ways that without shame-
Allow every part of your manhood to be revealed
In ways that tell your dick it is a weapon-
That no longer needs to be concealed
In ways that like a perfect composition-
Sends a message that is real and
Sings a harmony that in the depths of your soul,
You can feel

I want to touch you and kiss you in ways-
That say something you-
Aint neva even thought of before
In ways that say I not only love you-
But I also adore
In ways that say your wish is my command
And I'll do it with a smile-
Cause pleasing you is a hobby not a chore

I want to touch you and kiss you in ways that say-
I'll be with you in a mansion or
If we had to sleep on somebody's living room floor
In ways that say I'll carry 5 more of your seeds
In ways that say for someone's understanding-
You never have to plead
In ways that say your desire is-
My favorite book to read
In ways that say I'm your help mate from God-
So relief I'm here to breed
In ways that say till death do us part-
Cause for you I'd even let a bullet proceed

I want to touch you and kiss you in ways that say-
With me all days are better
In ways that cause you to become a millionaire-
As all your ideas transform to clever
In ways that say I'll hold it down-
No matter what the weather
In ways that say we have a tie that-
No man or woman can sever
I want to touch you and kiss you in ways that say-
FOREVER

So I run my fingers across your face
And patiently trace-
All the tear stains from your past;
Seeking to replace them with tenderness-
Cause I'm so blessed to be the last woman standing
My spirit is commanding the universe to-
Release you from the bondage of sorrow;
Giving you a first class ticket into a euphoric Tomorrow-
As I touch you and kiss you,
In ways

Vows

In sickness and in health
Whether poor or only with-
Wealth that comes from you soul
I'll step in wholeheartedly
Promise to never flee
Respect, Love and Support you through ALL
Both arms positioned to hold you after a fall
Help you get on track with prayer
Look at your back and I'm always there
Everything with you I share
I'll tuck our children in with bedtime stories;
Filled with the enthusiasm of our love-
Warmed by God's smile-
That shines down from above;
Granting US this chance
I stretch out my hand and ask-
May I have this dance . . . of life?
Euphoric tones cancel out-
Any strife that will come hither
Haters' Fed-Ex package unable to be delivered
Forsaking ALL others
Like that 1 pin on the bowling lane-
Refusing to be knocked over
Consistently using God as our shoulder-
As we grow older
And stronger
And happier
And wiser
Together

No other connection could be "Mo-Betta"
I sever the past and let it be true to its name
No wasting time with blame-
As we fight to change the game
Place my unconditional on your finger-
Will you wear it?
First gift we'll name Cayenne,
Second gift we'll name Cherish
Make no toy of your emotions,
Nor enter your world abrupt
My heart like the blood-
From old stab wounds reopened;
Spilling to let all spectators know what's up
Opening a new club called Commitment
Looking for a One Man band
No need for audition, just petition-
Your desire with the same reflection and
Bring forever into fruition
As truth walks out on a tight rope-
I know I'm gambling but
My emotions are not rambling
I counseled with the most high and cried-
Till sunrise hit my last tear-
Washing away any fears
It's clear

The end is near and there is work to be done
Want you close enough to pass the baton-
As we run this race;
Facing this world as one
Permanent place setting for your crown
Faith in me, not misguided
For all that you're about, I'm down
Not after premarital sex that-
Can get our spirits in a bind
Desire to join hands and dine with the divine
Taking US one day at a time
Won't leave you without security
Nothing to roam except-
The minutes on my cell phone
Pledged loyalty
Never changing our house from it's status of home
Life is too short to pretend
Can you join me in something-
Built on now, not then?
Forgetting everyone else's rules
Come dip in a pool of love redeemed
Meet me at the altar
And let's do the damn thing!

No Place Like Home

Being right, right now, is overrated
Apologies awaited always seem belated
But I'm going to rely on better late than not at all
So I call . . . to wipe the slate clean-
For anything that I've ever done or said,
That held demean
We're falling apart
First impressions wore off
Pieces rearranged within our hearts
Now the white flag ceremony has to start

And I'm asking you to go ahead and scold me-
But with your hypnotic smile-
That I haven't seen for a while
I've been tripping too so spank me;
With your pomegranate kisses
Dripping with warrior juices-
I truly miss and
Put me in check by grabbing me with-
Your strong man hands
Pulling me closer while giving me gentle reminders-
Of the rules of our school
Cuss me out with every stroke of your perfect stick-
That knows my favorite tricks and
After some hours
Oh yes, I said after some HOURS-
Our sweat's showers will cause our emotions to-
Tick
In sync
Then I blink and see you directing my pupils into-
The assurance of forgiveness . . .
YEAH, that's the business

Let's not waste any more time-
Avoiding each other on the phone and
Striving daily to prove one doesn't need the other-
Cause we can do it on our own
To others we both can roam but-
There's no place like home
So I click my heels with my-
Get out of relationship jail free card
And I click my heels with "I'm sorry"
And I click my heels with nothing else matters-
Cause I really care about you
And I click my heels because I'd be vexed-
If your name showed up on my caller ID as an EX-
Then a new heart I'd need to borrow;
As tomorrow would bring the rise of sorrow

So, Instead of "Whateva Nigga!"
I'll say baby I got you and push you to dream bigger
Instead of "Nigga yo hands aint broke!"
I'd enthusiastically hang on to every word you spoke
And massage one hand while,
The other changed the remote
Instead of "Aw not tonight Nigga, I'm tired!"
I'd wake up chanting how do you want it?
How do you want it?
How—Do-You—Want—It?
My King!
And fulfill even your unknown desires

In my absence you drank bitches
And appetized on hoes-
But you and I both know that was just for show
Those previews could never compare to our mold
This bond cannot be bought or sold
I'll fold my pride and follow your guide
No longer will true feelings hide
My new ears will abide and hold sacred your confide
I yearn your presence within and by my side-
Cause there's no place like home

I'm ready to take my position-
As your Nirvana Queen;
Standing to your right and down for everything-
Because when I think of home-
I think of a place where,
Your goodness is flowing
I've been around other men and shared their space
And things aren't the same-
Now I'm knowing
There's no place like home!
There's no place like home!
There's no place like home!
And you baby
You're home
And I'll never leave home again

1-2 1-2

I don't mean to disrespect you
But you did that on your own;
Coming up in my crib trying to break up my home
It may not always be happy but it is still mine
And you all up on my man-
While I'm out there on my grind
Check It: This is an Emergency Broadcast System-
Giving you some important facts,
Cause you must've missed them
He's my husband not my B-U-D-D-Y
We stood before God and said ride or die

Bitch Check
1-2 1-2
Bitch Check
1-2 1-2

Now let me break it down so it can be real simple-
Cause something must be wrong within your temple
I don't care about your little business date,
Personal you tried to make-
Just as long as you don't come up talking bout-
"My period is late"
And there aint gone be no tit for tat
See, this is my family-
So you can't bring a big enuf bat

You bragging cause you sucked his dick-
You dirty trick!
You just gave my jaws a vacation and
My pussy juices you licked-
Now aint dat a trip

News Flash: You can't take nobody's man-
He has to volunteer to leave
He may have got your nipples hard but-
It's to my bosom that he cleaves

Bitch Check
1-2 1-2
Bitch Check
1-2 1-2

You mize well get on da phone and
Call Tyrone-nika-
Cause the pitter patter in your heart-
Is about ta get weaker
I call you a bitch cause in ill ways;
Your actions speak a truth that says you don't-
Respect the sista I am-
Cause you knew he was married and
Still chose to play the wrong hand
Now I really don't want to hurt another sista-
But I will fuck you up
And don't act shocked like-
You didn't know what was up
Something casual aint what this union is about-
So as long as there's still love between us-
We'll forgive
And work our shit out

Bitch Check
1-2 1-2
Bitch Check
1-2 1-2

Our bond is not regular-
It comes with high wages
And unless you are Jesus Christ,
You can't afford to pay it
I'm painting a picture,
So it's not complicated
This is not territory that can be conquered cause-
He's my husband not some nigga I dated
You bitches develop this pride that is oh so twisted
Thinking you're the bomb with a man who's taken-
But the repercussions on this one-
You don't want to risk it
Like Jill Scott said-
You're getting in the way of what I'm feelin
And if I have to issue another warnin-
You gone be beggin for some healin-
That only comes from His mercy and His grace
Press your luck baby girl and
I'll put you close enough to see His face

Bitch Check
1-2 1-2
Bitch Check
1-2 1-2

Whatever you think you're sharing with him-
Is just a phase
And when it's all over you'll be lost in a daze
You buying him shit and think I'm not aware
I am, I just don't give a fuck or care, if you do more-
Cause he used your credit card and
Bought me and the kids-
Some fly shit at the store
He's like a Benz already sold but-
You keep trying to make a deposit
When you kissed him, you've literally kissed my ass-
You lesbian in the closet!
Bitch, a female dog, yeah, that's what you are
Braggin cause you in the game this far
But you're about to be on your back for reasons-
That aren't the same
You'll be telling your girlz how you got-
Knocked the fuck out and couldn't get up
My love for him is not soft like Charmin-
It's strong like Brawny and hangs on real tough

Bitch
Keep Bumping Into Chicks Husbands
Bitch
Trading in self-respect for some left over lovin
Bitch
Letting any man up in your oven
Bitch
Degrading yourself to the status of dime a dozen

Bitch Check
1-2 1-2
Bitch Check
1-2 1-2

What it do?

1-2 1-2 REVELATION

As I sit here thinking about my man and you
I realized that I wasn't only dealing with one Bitch
NO, in fact, there were two
So I'm going to get off your tip and
Take a moment to address the BIGGER Bitch
That would be the man with whom I share a bed
Yes, the BIGGER bitch is the man to whom I wed
See you are the one who made a commitment to me
And without any consent of mine-
You changed our problem of 1+1 is 2 to = 3
I'm showing anger towards the other woman but-
It's with you that my anger should be
Although she did pursue you,
Knowing your state of married;
It's you who met me at the altar and
Our vows, you were to always carry
You BITCH ASS NIGGA! . . .
Tricking our union off for a temporary treat
I opened my heart and saved you a special seat
It's not just me but also our children-
Who will suffer defeat
Trust and believe as I close the door behind us-
Your heart will form irregular beats
Slipping off my wedding ring as I see beyond the veil
Lit up a cigarette
And watched my favorite scene from
Waiting to Exhale

My girl Bernadine looked at the car filled with-
Her husband's clothes and shoes that had burned
"It is trash" was what she helped the fireman confirm
As I took a puff of a cigar I thought of the famous Loraina;
Looking for the dick she had cut off her husband-
Had the police goin insane . . . a
I also remember the story of the burning bed
"Hell hath no fury like a woman scorn"
Is what I believe the flames read
Why am I taking your bitch ass on my trip down Memory lane?
Well I'm thinking of all the times we made love and
All the times in that bitch, you came

Lame is the image I'm seeing of you
Perhaps I should brush up on my arts n crafts
And decorate yo dick wit some hot glue
Ooooh
Bet that hurt just to hear
Here's a box of my favorite dildos;
You can shove em up your rear
BITCH!

Ladies,
Don't be that bitch
Don't fight that bitch
Don't stay with that bitch

HOLD UP! HOLD UP!

I'm not leaving . . .
Get yo shit
And get the fuck out-
Cause I see what it is that you about
And I aint the one who broke up the wedding party
This is my house bitch . . .
You betta ask somebody!

CUSTOM MADE

A Poem For Tanya

I was asked to tell what La Tanya meant to us,
Her friends
Yes, that's the tradition of funerals
We get up and tell what we are feeling, one by one
But quite frankly,
That's an expressive task to complete-
While one is living;
Which means-
It should have already been done
Tanya is fine and she is in a better place
She finished her race and
Has gone to Heaven to claim her space
We are the ones messed up down here-
In this hell on earth still;
With an emptiness in our hearts that-
Only strength from God and good memories can fill
No, of course I'm not saying it's okay
I'm just gonna take some time and be real today
It's not okay that a 21 year old young woman is gone
And we are left here to figure out how to move on

It's not okay that a sista who was working,
Going to school and trying;
Was suddenly trapped in her Honda . . . dying
It's not okay to feel like you lost part of your soul
And are no longer whole
You've developed a feeling of powerlessness
And it won't let you rest

It's not okay what happened on Wednesday
And you may have a "Why Lord!" attitude-
For the next 365 days
Right now, La Tanya cries out . . .
Remember the song I used to sing the solo to?
Just Let Jesus Fix It For You
With that said
I'm going to do what I think I should-
By expressing to you what I think La Tanya would

Tania: Like a sister, always trying to set me straight when I was naïve. And taught me all the tricks on how to make sure your man won't leave.

Stacy: You used to fry, dye, and lay to the side my hair. I'll save you a styling booth in Heaven and I'll be waiting in the chair.

Dawn: Remember the time we went to the Golden Tail and I was on the dance floor? As you watched me, you thought, look at that church girl go! You said Tanya I didn't think a lil church girl could do all the moves you were showing. I said Dawn, I learned those moves in the choir. Christians have SOL girl! You aint knowing? Dawn, I will miss all the good times we had. You were a genuine friend and for that I am glad.

Chris: We shared so much together I don't know where to begin. I want you to know that I always loved you and despite everything I'm glad we remained friends.

Alvin: Tell lil Alvin and lil Jordan how wonderful and fine cousin Tanya is. And tell them I'll put in a good word for them with God if they behave and be good kids.

_T.J.:_ You were truly a good friend. I'll never forget how you sent me money when I was at Oakwood cause you know a sista was broke back then.

Gerald: I'll miss those little outings we used to have . . . like the time we took Brianna to The Reef restaurant. It'll be even better when you get up here cause they got everything you could want.

Mommy: I already told everybody that you sing a mean soprano so you're signed up for the choir on high. Don't forget to bring me some of those mouth-watering homemade rolls cause I told the angels you'd make a dozen x 25.

Daddy: I know I probably gave you few gray hairs and maybe a lil strife. So to make up for it I saved you a spot in the choir too, for I remember how you used to sang with the group Breath of Life.

Clay: I know I used to tease you about not being worldly or wild anymore, but I had the deepest respect for you behind closed doors. Please don't give up on God's work and don't let your spirit die. I already promised the angels a minister of music so don't make me look like I lied.

Pastor
Dawson: Uncle Billy, you were my best example of Christianity. Because of you I learned I could have fun and still be what God wanted me to be.

To the rest of my family and friends
Don't be upset if I didn't call you by name
Yall know you only have this church for an hour
And Christian or not, they will kick you out just the same!

The "Going Home" Celebration for Latanya Allen

The Preacher's Prayer

Here is the story never been told;
About the man behind the pulpit-
Who seems spiritually bold
It doesn't matter if you're young or old;
The call to ministry always comes with a toll
The closer you get to God-
The more mess unfolds,
So through my prayer life-
I'm gonna let you scroll
I'm just a man from the Chicago streets
I struggle daily just to keep up my heartbeat
Sometimes I catch the heat for others defeat
This often happens when I tend your sheep
I strive to sow better seed-
So I meet every need;
But I'm still left to bleed-
Cause some flock didn't like the feed
So Lord I turn to you with plea-
Cause you remember being human like me

The man behind the clothe your people can't see
I don't mean to offend but I hurt just like them,
That's why I-

Shout, shout, let it all out
These are the things that I pray about
All night long
I'm talking to you on the throne

Many times I have tears I need you to wipe-
Because some saints choose to mistreat my wife
She's the reflection of your love;
Essence of my life-
For her happiness, I'd pay the highest price
I preached How To Receive What You Believe;
Then came to a point of-
Taking permanent leave from the pulpit-
To achieve the respect for the woman-
To whom I cleave
To my need you did heed indeed and
Told your angels to flee down to earth
And see about your boy who was deeply annoyed
And no longer tolerant of being toyed
The angel said "William you can't quit"
And I knew this cause Inglewood was-
Still a pile of unsettled S—
Should I resort to the snort-
Just to sort all the troubles of the day-
Till my pain goes away?
As my spirit man starts to decay;
There's no time for delay on-
Hearing what you say;
So on my knees I pray and I

Shout, shout, let it all out
These are the things that I pray about
All night long
I'm talking to you on the throne

Now don't believe the hype;
It's not easy to win the preacher's fight
To save a soul we live our lives on strike
Try not to doubt in the dark-
What God told us in the light
Impatiently I wait like a fisherman with bait;
As I re-learn How To Achieve A New Level Of Faith
New hearing I must cultivate;
So I listen to the Holy Spirit reiterate
Yes, I'm a preacher but I'm Hu-Man
Feels like I'm in the devil's frying pan
Daily facing battles from a different KKKlan
Only survive because it's God's plan
I want to fulfill what I'm yearning-
But the Lord brings me back to a place of learning . . .
Before my sermon and
With the people my life can positively turn
Back in the day I did a lot of stuff-
Stealing, swearing, or taking a puff-
Things boyz do in the hood when they're growing up
One time I got burned real tough
And said alright, that's enough . . .
Lord I want to be filled with the right stuff
Don't want no harm to come to, my child-ren-
Because of what I did back then
Drops of tears in my eyes as I realize;
My son through marriage-
Views my manhood as a prize
All this time I thought I was just used and abused
After betrayal of too many friends,
I almost blew a fuse
But you cleaned me up enough-
That my new life he'd choose
So Lord I'll gladly take the fall for all of his sins;
If you just let him be the best of men . . . So I

Shout, shout, let it all out
These are the things that I pray about
All night long
I'm talking to you on the throne

Shout, shout, let it all out
These are the things that I pray about
All night long
I'm talking to you on the throne

Yes, I'm a preacher
But I'm Hu-Man
Yes, I'm a preacher
But I'm Hu-Man
Understand?

Appreciation Service for Pastor William Dawson

God Said Now

I've worn more than one wedding band
Given more than one person my heart and hand
Built new homes from old promises made
Later saw them demolished-
As they took while I gave
I almost went so far as to say-
That God didn't even care;
Since I was allowed to frequent the rode of despair
Was my line busy or was I out at the store?
Cause I don't seem to recall good love-
Knocking at my door
My pain was insane
All men and women are the same
I didn't want to seal my heartbreak again
On my knees, I'd plead, God, Father, are you there?
Almighty King!
You turned water into wine-
Surely you can fix this thing
What I could not express was transparent to God
He knew I was two steps from the edge-
So He gave His angels a nod
I suddenly felt an unusual presence in my spirit
Burdens were lifted and relief, I was near it
A slide show began playing of God's plan
See, He revealed some things that-
I did not understand
My life had not been a tornado of bad people
And marriage

I've been in training for a true happiness carriage
The arguments gave me the compassion to-
Help you let your guard down and heal
I'm familiar with being ignored so-
I'll make sure that those things you will never feel
The loneliness gave me the strength to be Monogamous-
Not allowing temptation to rule-
Because without you there's no US
And solely loving you is a must
The many shifts in my physical form-
Prepped me for all the changes-
A relationship can bring
Our union will succeed because I will love you-
Through ANYTHING
And yes, disappointment just exercised and
Strengthened my faith;
So if ever our attitudes are not in sync-
I'll pray and patiently wait
Every single tear I cried-
God held in a cloud above and
Over 25 years later he caused that cloud to burst
And shower me with your love
Sweethearts before high school,
Such a long time ago
How we ever grew apart-
I don't really know
BUT how we came back together-
Now that is a story to be told
We're both 60 years old and
God gave us new joy to unfold

Oh your smile is my favorite song
And I've appreciated you;
Even those things that were wrong
You took time to remove my mountain of distrust
And like no other carpenter-
Carved in me a sacred lust
You took me on a never-ending cruise of laughter
Now I caress the meaning of-
Happily-Ever-After
In comfort I shared with you-
What others made me hide
Your California ID reads-
My Recovery Guide
You gave back what I reported stolen-
From my inner gates
You're my Soul Mate
My Goal Mate
You're my You Complete Me
And make Me Whole Mate
We . . . used to complain and ask God why or how?
But when in each other's presence-
All we can do is say WOW!
Tuxedo and Wedding Gown-
Getting ready to exchange vows
We're reminded of God's favor because-
Instead of NO or WAIT
This time
This time
God Said Now

The Wedding of Bruce (Daddy) &Charlotte Hall

Take A Piece Of Me

Committed, Dedicated, Encourager, Lover of people,
Genuine, Intuitive, Warm, Studious, Teacher,
Never idle, Believer, Friend, Husband, Father to all, Elder,
Praiser, Giver, Right hand man, Protector, Strength, Laughter,
Energetic, Soulful, Musician
These things combined is what George Turpeau defines

He lived his life in a permanent phase;
striving to live right and raise the praise,
with each new age
His success caused the devil to go into a rage
and soon increased his bounty hunter's wage
Brother Turpeau looked the devil straight in the eye
and declared I fear not what you try to make happen
God put something inside me and its survival has a patent

Brother Turpeau was REAL and
admitting his shortcomings was his fashion;
in hopes that all who witnessed would copy his passion
During church service Brother Turpeau would-
jump out his seat, grab the mic, and plead
"There's something I've just gotta say"
He now needs someone to speak through;
so I'll let him use me today
This thing called life is serious folks!
No time left to play
Get yourself in order or there'll be hell to pay
A funeral has little to do with the life now gone-
but a lot to do with how those left behind will carry on

In one moment, the twinkling of an eye,
you'll lift your head and see the Savior arrive
FEEL THIS MOMENT
Not in worry for me because-
I have no question about the final destination-
of my spirit man's body
FEEL THIS MOMENT
Yawn until it hurts because-
a wakeup call is a precursor of the changes,
for which you must thirst
No tears for me except joy
God already said Well done George-
here's your ticket to the Heavenly Club Savoy
I went on in, then moved up close
Oh mercy be!
Coltrane is introduced by the angelic host
Wait a minute, is that someone weeping?
Okay you didn't hear what I said-
you better stop sleeping cause
my words are about to get deepened
Right now I need you to shift your emotions and
realize my work is not over-
I just got transferred from earth to the sky
Oh Ira Nell, my sweet baby
I know you're mad I left but-
I had to answer God's call
and you know He knows what's best
Woman, I want you to undoubtedly know that-
when you entered a room;
you commanded my insides to glow
My children, I know you'll hurt for a while but-
never forget you were my smile

Alright, alright, I'm getting off track
Now to the matter at hand, I must get back
Times a ticking so I don't have long
I began a composition but I need you-
to help me finish my last song
God wants you to play your life in the right key;
so before my spirit ascends to Heaven I want you to-
Take A Piece Of Me
When you walk by my casket-
don't make it long and drastic
Know that I lived my life-
for something that would outlast it
Jesus died so that you'd be free and
He gave me transferable strength-
so touch my body and get your survival feed
Take a piece of me and plant new seeds-
to continue my work of trying to help people in need
Take a piece of me and blow it like a horn;
making sure you give love to these young people-
whose hearts have been torn
Oh **Take a piece of me** and
share it with the pianos variations
and change this nation
Take a piece of me with the boldness of the trombone
and visit the sick and shut in,
bringing life into their very bones
Oh **Take a piece of me** and work it out like a sax-
to smooth things wherever you go and attitudes-
have reached their max
Take a piece of me and beat it like a drum-
so that education can be great for ALL and
not just for some

Oh **Take a piece of me** living life to the fullest-
completely out of your norm
Take a piece of me and hold on-
so you can make it to Heaven and
see me and Lionel Hampton perform

The "Going Home" Celebration of
Brother George Turpeau

The Perfect Blend

You palmed my soul
The piece that fit the last space on the puzzle
Making me whole
Placed my uncertainty in an uncomfortable hold
Even the tone of your voice said
Making sure I shed no more tears was your goal
You Gave Me Life

Could God be this good to grant me
What I didn't even know I should be wishing
Life seemed okay all by myself
So I was convinced that happiness wasn't missing
Then you came along, my international anthem-
Delivering patience with every kiss
Euphoric sentiment conducting my insides christening
After each day with you-
I have treasured reminiscing
Cause You Gave Me Life

Then we unveiled the life of our son
Who is our greatest prize
Better than all the gifts brought by
The three men who were wise
Seems too good to be true but
The Father cannot lie
Today, Augusto is the groom and
Portia is the bride
From day 1 sharing a surreal connection
Painting a portrait that reflects Heaven's perfection
Angels rejoicing like it was the resurrection
From this day forward we breathe
A bond of affection
Cause You Gave Me Life

Sunshine told the raindrops to
Shake hands with defeat
My heart opened up and
You took a front row seat
If ever a sequel to my life-
Our chapters I'd play on repeat
No doubt you are the one for me
Cause you make me complete
California and Argentina-
We've been loving from a distance
I like how you're exactly what I'm not
Our opposites make sense and
My feelings for you are not wrong so
No need for repentance
To anything that would forfeit our union-
I'd put up the strongest fence
Now my heart resides within the clouds
That decorate the sky-
Stretched out just beneath the Heavens-
Sending a text message invitation
To a rendezvous of E-ter-ni-ty
Cause You Gave Life To Me

Life so I can
Live **I**nfinitively **F**reed from **E**xcuses
Lounge **I**n **F**irm **E**ncouragement
Loathe **I**n **F**lowing **E**cstasy
Linger **I**ntently **F**orever **E**lated
LIFE

I looked in your eyes and they said
God sent you
You held my hands and I felt secure
That with you it would be a whole new world
You've shown me all the things-
My other relationships lacked
I'm even speaking in a different tongue cause
You Gave It Back

Me devolviste
Una vida del dulzura
Una vida de paz
Una vida de alegría
Una vida insaciable
Una vida irremplazable
Indiscutible
Desinhibida
Inobjetable
Tu amor unconditional

You gave it back to me
Life sweet
Life peace
Life joy
Life insatiable
Life irreplaceable
Undisputable
Uninhibited
Unobjectable
Your unconditional love

Today I vow to spend the rest of my life
Writing you a thank you letter with my smile
Caressing your emotions
with my tenderness
Fondling your dreams with my understanding
And fulfilling your every desire corner to corner
Within the 4 walls of whatever offspring of-
Construction we convert into our lover's arena
You traveled and left your country for me-
Now whatever you need is my subpoena

As my subconscious mind searched for love
My conscious mind fought to
Distinguish reality from fiction-
As infatuation is a similar addiction
So at times, I wondered what REAL love **smells** like
Real love smells pure and unique
Like your natural aroma
That keeps me in a hypnotic coma
I wondered what real love **feels** like
Real love feels like the crocheting of our skins-
Till reaching a liquid end and
Even with the absence of penetration-
Still leaves a speechless sensation
Oh I wondered what real love **tastes** like
Real love tastes like the seasoning of salvation-
Replacing everything bad with splendid restoration
I wondered what real love **sounds** like
Real love sounds like a dead silence-
Accompanied by deep stares to the soul-

That whisper Sade's Sweetest Taboo or
Kilometros For a Love Song-
That made me save the last dance for you
I wondered what real love **looks** like
Real love looks like a sunrise silhouette of 2-
Lying side by side in the morning-
On sheets saturated with lover's dew,
Pillows that spell I only have eyes for you,
A comforter filled with fabric that reads-
You're the Queen or King of my heart and
A headboard engraved with-
Till death do US part

We've seen each other's worst and best-
Gone through thick and thin
Now I'm sure that real love is US
Because Portia and Augusto are
The **Perfect Blend**

For the Wedding of Augusto and Portia Bruno

The Dream of Bri

As little girls we dream of turning Sweet 16
Anticipating our paths taking a turn into the vast sea-
of which all women are deemed
We gather with family and friends and
party till our heads are spinning
And then the spinning stops and there we see it . . .
LIFE . . .
and who we really are
A princess like Brianna who is a natural star
What will she do now to raise the bar amongst her peers?
Erasing the many fears that growing up-
can paint on our canvas
On the planet of women she's now landed;
agreeing to abandon some of her childish ways
and moving on up to better days-
where she will give the DJ a list of songs,
that display her new spirit
Asking questions so she can get clear
Who am I?
And
What makes me free?
What will I do after high school and college?
And
With what man will I be?
Will I have the same friends?
Will I get a place of my own?
What all will come with this package called being grown?
I must water all the seeds that my female ancestors have sown
Have a demeanor that is a banner that says;
I have standards and if you want a piece of this "cookie"-
you will have to put a ring on it

And if we get into a quarrel, it's not okay to hit because-
the one who sits above says self I should respect and love-
allowing others to do no less
Be strong and be my own person
Live this life freely,
not thru what others rehearsed or envision
Let God be the incision that cuts thru all the SH—
-IT won't be the way the devil thought
My greatness stems from the cross
and can't be sold or bought
My way already paved
Not a slave to any environment
Looking to one day be the one they call BOSS;
because I'm the one who's doing the hiring
If I keep looking to that which is higher;
I will connect with my true beauty
Forgetting what haters said they see,
Knowing all that's really voluptuous
came from deep within me, **Bri**
Sweet 16 having a dream;
not realizing God already spoke it into existence-
Sent His angels down to be my assistants
Sweet 16, watching the map of my dreams-
being drawn on that same canvas-
where my pain used to have a reservation
All bullets dodged cause God was the preservation of me
till this very moment . . . Sweet 16-
not just celebrating another theme-
but celebrating a dream set free

For the Sweet 16 party of Brianna Murphy-Glenn

191

Still Holding On

An unchanging hand I took hold of a long time ago
So regardless of the test results;
God's reality will show
With that said, today, I resign from-
my position of heavy weight fighter;
cause I serve a risen Savior and
I'm now majoring in rest while looking up higher
Fire shut up in my weary bones
For the smell of sweet PEACE
I've got a fierce love Jones
Some people see me with eyes of pity because;
I'm not dressed for life's usual party-
But they must understand that this aint the first time-
that I've been knocked off my ass,
as if I had drank 6 bottles of Bacardi
Hardly new to this game
I've rode through many storms and
suffered immense pain
Sometimes just over my family, but its all the same
Lame became the branches of our tree;
from encounters with rough patches on the road of-
trying to do right cause I used to do wrong
Yet there was a constant in the hand I held that said;
I could always sing a new song-
If I let FAITH be more than my private dancer
Prolonged has been the visit of this cancer;
Probing me with a torment that even would have—knocked
the twin towers down faster
Death cast her net, seeking to gather those who are-
spiritually precocious and refuse to wander
No attitude of "Why me? or How could you Lord?"
do I take time to ponder

Fonder I've grown for the voice
that speaks from up yonder;
saying take my hand Lisa and
GET UP!
Cause you're made from a stock that's
so much stronger
Etched across your chest in bold letters is the word-
BELIEVE
Cause every time someone let you down;
you put 100 in me who you knew could reprieve
Take my hand Lisa and
GET UP!
For this sickness is not your true_identity
It is just a means for someone of a weaker fabric-
to witness the truth of the trinity;
then begin to live their lives to reach
the land beyond infinity
Take my hand Lisa and
GET UP!
For the book of Jeremiah is not a liar
I have plans for you in this very moment;
so block out any talk of retire
Simply desire my Word's conviction-
above the restriction of this infliction
and the harvest thereof is one that no man-
could reap from selling any addiction-
cause my love for you is not fiction . . . . **Lisa**
As I heard God shower me with
His blessed assurance
I-GOT-UP!
With the absence of the usual sway
God said although I am made in His image;

I didn't have to wait 3 days-
High price already paid;
Laid the foundation for my resurrection
and if I be an X-Men then my Last Stand will be firm in Him
Knowing that no matter how many times
I am struck down;
I will get back up again
Won't break-
Just bend the rules
That deem a person in this stage of cancer-
to be completely out of fuel
But as God fills me up to see-
the beauty of yet another dawn
I would ask that you pass me-
My earrings
Lipstick
And shoes
Cause I Am
Still Holding On

For Lisa Wilkes aka Auntie Lisa/Diva

For Olivene

I got up early this morning-
thinking of **You** while stretching a bit,
then I had an epiphany and clearly knew-
that I was too old for this shit!
It's been fun . . .
Hell, I would even beg to say fantastic but-
you want a beautiful booty call and
that's got my morals engaged in gymnastics
60 years plus and I'm past this game-
that creates lesson for little girls to learn
You want to frequent my residence to-
secure your manhood by the measure of my squirm
Earned is what I failed to require of my goods but;
the heart has a beat of its own causing it to feel-
things whether or not is should
I would have treated you like a King but-
you couldn't act right long enough
for me to show this
and my feelings don't have 3 more days-
so here's your TODAY notice
I resign from being the bone that you could count on
I've got children who have children;
so I don't need one on loan
I'm looking for a Ribbon in the Sky-
while you're working hard at telling me good lies
Lord knows I've tried to justify this situation but;
I can no longer betray my long fought for emancipation
Awakened and soul shaken cause-
when the words I Love You left my mouth,
there was no faking-
So I know I will truly miss you-

But I am a woman who strives to be a true Christian And
every moment I indulge in this madness;
God is watching, not only listening
In the lifestyle that you've chosen I will not meddle-
but by the same token baby;
against the commitment that I need-
I will not settle
Don't tell me "Aw it aint like that baby"
trying to buy yourself time
as you fuck with my memory
Just get yo shit and walk away cause-
you and things of the past-
are now the ones with the symmetry
Like the water Jesus turned to wine-
I get sweeter as I grow older
Understand the cookie jar is now closed-
so buy yourself a good blanket-
cause it's about to get colder.

LIFE LESSONS
PART II

The Dance

One night I saw Courage and Strength dance
Courage being the one without fear;
stepped out on the dance floor, swaying her hips-
in a manner that caused all things negative to disappear
Strength was posted on the wall nearby;
displaying his firmness and power-
while watching every move of Courage and
preparing to be there in her darkest hour
Courage shook her thang and waved her hands;
as she danced to the tune of freedom that was-
absent from ancestor slaves
In a blink, Courage had to switch up her moves as-
this other dancer named tribulation began to-
crowd her more and more
The DJ being in tune with the scene,
played a song called danger-
as remnants of sweat hit the dance floor
with every beat
Strength who was cognizant of opposition
And therefore had never left his post;
pushed off the wall and danced over to Courage-
to aid her when she needed him most
Strength grabbed Courage by the hand,
with a durability that cancelled any questions
of capability and
Courage held on to Strength and they danced
And danced and
danced until Courage knew that Strength was her ego's alter-
so keeping him close would minimize future falter;
by those whom would seek to halt her

So she gripped him tighter-
as if both hands were hers and they danced
And danced and
danced and danced and danced and danced
And danced-
until they tapped out the words-
It's the God in me.

The 2nd Secret

I've got a secret but I can't keep it to myself
It is the epitome of wealth

Life was meant to be abundant in all areas;
so walking around existing as a broken soul-
should be much scarier than-
using this Miracle that I've whipped up;
for you to spread on your bread
Cut off your old head or you'll end up dead,
without reasoning
The Secret tells you to minimize what's painful
and maximize what's pleasing
Don't hold others responsible for
making you feel good
God gave you a make up that says you,
yourself, could
We all have an imagination
which is a powerful stencil
and if used to its fullest potential;
can raise our emotional and
our mental to levels that-
elevate what scientists can't calculate;
but are left to debate its awesomeness
As monumental as the very creation;
needing a 7th day just to rest
Recognize what you don't want in life;
without letting it become your focus-
Then concentration thereof will just;
breed a bunch of hocus pocus
I've just recently woke up from my recurring nightmare;
that's how I know this
You are a magnificent Creator and Creation;
sent here to flip the nation-
with a lift that can only spawn form your gift

"Life is an Infinite Field of Unfolding Possibilities;"
where everything in it is REAL energy
We all come from families that are dysfunctional;
but God is always punctual in His healing
and since He's the greater that is within me;
I can exude different feelings and start-
peeling back my Family's original mold,
with no regret-
but with a little something extra
so they too can forget;
all the lies they were told with marked down
price tags-
on which our hopes were almost sold
What you Resist-Persists;
so list all the things you do want and
all the negative stuff won't continue to haunt you when
you sleep as it peeps;
the phenomenal scent of a woman or man-
In the beginning, The Most High spoke-
that makes the devil choke and
no one else can revoke;
If you keep not just telling, but living by the rules-
of The Secret, to its peak
and the psychology of failure says-
you are not a liar but a future teller;
who determines what brand of wine-
will be stocked in your cellar

What you say will push play in your tomorrow
and that's a reality you need to purchase not borrow
Success often brings about the pressure of reproduction,
which creates fear-
but tell success to always be near you like-
a lover that has taken you;
to a level you can't even explain
and you are not separated but divorced from failure;
as it had you traveling through the wrong terrain-
with nothing worth passing on to gain
The Secret requires that you listen and learn
Don't be so full of knowledge
that the path to more of it;
like the wrong bridges you burn
But always turns into sweet cream;
that releases your impossible dreams

Life is an ocean filled with variations of dichotomies
My ying and your yang misused can have;
the outcome of a not so victorious phlebotomy-
more painful than sodomy-
but probably through the sharing of **The Secret** . . .
others won't have to suffer as this info is given freely And
represents a subliminal buffer
Get off your slave wagon
What you imagine will breathe as fierce as fire from a dragon
And you filing a disclaimer of all the bad things you tagging;
cause this is the Law of Attraction

Conduct your own Visual Motor Rehearsal
Instead of seeing yourself last . . . see yourself 1st
and get out of the low self-esteem hearse
And embrace your spirit's worth-
like a new seed that once planted;
will know growth is coming and
put out a welcome mat
As a matter of fact . . .
We defeat ourselves because we can't grasp-
the reality of "New World" manifestation-
but **The Secret** requires that we let seeing
And being-
become our new habituation
The how will show up clearly in
the commitment of the what
Let your mind autopilot your destiny
and a flight that can't be redirected;
will be what's up
Retrieve, Conceive, Believe, Achieve . . .
no longer Bereave your own death-
cause you inhaled The Secret and
then exhaled what's best
The Secret requires that you be the director
and not the audience
As "Humans" will always try to cast you for-
the leading role of fraudulence
Take time to spectate but know-
how to differentiate the information you receive
All is precious BUT
you must know which to hold as truths
and which to put to rest

How bad do you want to be happy and free?
How bad do you want a change in your life-
you can taste and see?
How bad do you want to stop hitting
those bumps in the road?
How bad do you desire to be
the next heroic story told?
How bad do you want to step out of the box-
that came with no directions?
How bad do you want to understand and
not be perplexed?
And
How bad do you want without sex to receive-
the benefits of a satisfied erection?
How bad do you want to reek of God's perfection?
How bad do you want to go higher so others too can reach it?
How bad, just how bad, do you want to get
The Secret?
of which I'm speaking

**Somebody told me a secret and
I can't keep it to myself
I have to share it because
I don't want my soul to get rich all by itself!**

R.S.V.P.

This goes out to all my Sistas
Especially my young Sistas
We've got to R.S.V.P.
Reserve Some Virtue Please

What are you trying to prove?
What you wear is a path you choose
Precious things that decision could
cause you to lose
From tops to bottoms;
It's all a fashion statement
But depending on how your rock it;
It can be degrading

I see you walking by with your skirt
stretched up to the sky
and your blouse open like the 2nd parting of
the Red Sea
and you cheesin talking bout "Look, I have these"
Then a brotha comes and sweetly puts you down
and with twisted mentality
You think that puts a jewel in your crown;
but it actually made it fall down

All of your physical exposure is
just a false promotion;
that has absolutely nothing to do with love
and devotion

A precious union is about what's on the inside;
not how many times you let someone cut the price between
your thighs
A brotha will take your treats
if you put them out there
A second visit means the treat was good;
not that he really cares

You strive daily to be the new hottie or
young breezy-
Elegant or easy, sexy or sleazy,
it all has similar lines;
but you must break the code on trap compliments
or you'll end up in an uncomfortable bind

Don't let a brotha call your house to late
Always patronizing Block Buster;
never out on a date
He'll pressure you for sex
to prove your feelings for him
and you'll give in if the right things
aren't rooted within
And he won't share the punishment for your sin
and if you come up pregnant
he'll be gone with the wind

He'll jeopardize your life
trying to sex you without a glove
Saying "We don't need that baby
cause this is real love"
My opinions on you I don't mean to shove;
but if you're looking for that unconditional-
it only comes from above

I'm not like some nigga who wants to hurt you-
Just a Sista who cares and must alert you;
cause somehow you keep misplacing your virtue-
forgetting you were a Queen from birth
You think I'm here to just criticize;
but I want to help you stop getting caught up-
in the smooth man's lies
I've been involved in a twin demise
and for the pursuit of happiness-
Self-compromised
Still live a portion of my life trying to survive;
what I need to hide
So, some of what I've said may seem abrupt;
but I come at you like this-
because your eyes are wide shut
Sista, let me help remove your pain;
so you never have to be just another trick again

I wanna tell you about a friend of mine
She breeds a countenance that has
an all weather shine
Her name is Virtue
But I call her V
She is the truth of what every woman should be
Virtue goes against the grain of the lame;
who scout out blind fame
She's not the same
She has royal game

Virtue believes in bringing sexy back;
without being on her back
and that's what others lack
Who said Self Respect and Self Preservation
wasn't sexy?
Those people who aren't spiritually free-
or those people who don't understand-
the pleasure of mystery
Virtue is in high demand
Cause she melts in your thoughts-
not in your hands

Virtue is that woman who loves to have a good time-
but with classy array
and when others are in trouble;
she'll drop on her knees and pray
Some women get in the same position;
but without nothing to say-
just letting him have his way;
on any given day-
while listening to Shirley Murdock's
As We Lay
Virtue wears jeans that look like
they were custom fit;
for all her trunk's junk-
but her seams stay together
and her coochie can still breathe

Her bust is accentuated naturally;
because she got in line twice when-
God was passing them out
Not because she has them hanging all about;
like flyers to a party
When she struts her skirt shifts;
so her legs show-
but she never hikes it for
the intentional audition of a ho-
cause she knows that her surprise;
is not for everyone's eyes
When she dances she sways her hips;
but does not let every Tom, Dick, Gary, and Larry-
slip between them to converse with her other lips

NO, she can resist the invitation;
Camouflaged with the devil's decoration-
Saying "You are cordially invited to be my fool"
Virtue turns this invitation down;
because she actually paid attention in school
and she is governed by higher rules

Her primary physician is God;
So in special waters she trods
and when passing she gets respectful nods
She's the one men seek but think they'll never find
Her inner beauty convinces them to leave their past behind
and the mere aroma of her character;
causes them to change their minds-
every time

Virtue taught me that I'm worth more than any treasure
Virtue says that I was not made just for temporary pleasure
Virtue teaches me that my wealth cannot be calculated
Virtue teaches me that even though I made mistakes-
It's not to late and
Virtue teaches me that my value is beyond appraisal
Virtue teaches me that I can do all things because-
my God is able
Virtue teaches me that my merchandise is good
and I don't have to keep slumming in low Self Esteem's hood
Virtue teaches me to practice lovin Who—I-Am'
And-
Respect for Spirit, Soul, and Body, should be on command
Virtue says that I've been forgiven for what-
I've already done and
I can continue the legacy of Proverbs 31

There is nothing that anyone can make you do
God allows you to make your own decisions
so its up to you
Today, you can tell your past you're through
and tomorrow morning-
wake up with the agenda of Virtue

Sistas, we've got to R.S.V.P.
Reserve Some Virtue Please

Values

I value what Aretha Franklin sang about,
just simple respect
I value not having to write a bounced check
I value the clear face of honesty
I value the things that bring about
peace and harmony
I value the very form of my son
and daughter's smile
I value those days when I can
go to the spa for a while
I value each day that God lets me breathe
I value the takeover of serenity that
subtracts my pet peeves
I value every time I take my position
on a platform or stage
I value the beauty I'm increasing with age
I value the sweet taste of my mama's
monkey bread-
that never made it to the day's end
I value being able to take vacations and
just have some fun every now and then
I value forgiveness regardless of repentance
I value God's unconditional love that-
let me end my past's sentence
I value ALL God has put within me
I value the opportunity to share my experiences
and knowledge that can set others free

Elephant Man Mentality

What does it mean to be a human being?
What does it mean to do the right thing?
What does it mean to be a true Christian?
Do we judge each other by God's facts or
our deceptive pupil's fiction?
What is the deepened meaning of the words
sung throughout the golden rule?
When there's a battle of good and evil before us
who tends to win the duel?
Cruelty takes center stage as we patronize our-
need to hide our realities that would otherwise;
cause us to be brave
Immortal slaves as we have allowed our right-
spirits to be chained
Look up one day to a ledger that says-
we have no profitable gain
Shame how we get drunk off the misfortune
of another
Countless morbid characters
in an intoxicating plague-
yet to be discovered
A spool started back to the days B.C.
Auction blocks haven't been dismissed
So many people still aren't free
Sadly only the one fashioned with chains-
understands their dilemma
and the one hands-free,
has exchanged the original agenda
Does the intricacy of others bring you joy sustained
or are they simply a means to
keep yours out of range?
Hangings aka lynching's are still in plain view

Now there's exclusion of white sheets as-
others help arrange the strange fruit
Dreams swinging in the stenched breeze
While you're taking part in communion;
I hope this moment will freeze.
I seize this opportunity to beg forgiveness for us all
You have to let Adam and Eve off the hook when-
you keep setting up your own falls
Call waiting-
pick it up-
It is God!
You will be destroyed long before this earth-
if this path you continue to trod
Re-focus yourselves and seek Him more-
than how to entertain man
He's given you a 2nd, 3rd, 4th or 100th time-
to stick to His plan
Everyone you encounter is God in another form
When you mistreat them,
it's actually His flesh you've torn
Warnings come but are often not repeated
Heed the call of the one who on high is firmly seated
There's no easy maintenance of the things-
from the cross He envisioned
The Father's heart breaks for His children-
as they major in soul incisions
Collisions are rampant cause
you don't understand the fact that
He made you opposites with a main similarity
Embracing the God in you-
is the beginning of your clarity

Scary it can be to love to real you;
the live scan that would go to the grave if-
you could seal your conscience with super glue
Few look at all they are because of-
the painful branding from their past's scars
Pride should be exempt if keeping others down-
was how you earned wealth thus far
Bar raisers is the image you inherited
If you take the other painting from in front of that Then;
self-love will breed success and you can carry it
Your roots of self-hatred, yes it's time to bury it
Acceptance of your fellow man,
it's high time you marry it
It's not easy, in the winter,
to have someone remove your covers-
but God is sending out a tweet that reads
Love One Another!

In the Bank

I see you!
You've got plenty of "Bling" on your teeth
and on your tank
But seriously baby,
I need to know
Do you have any money in-the-bank?
Oh no!
I aint nothing like a gold digger-
I just need to know if you can-
afford my back if life pulls a trigger;
cause bigger things like the future-
is what my mind is on

See at some point, my heart,
will have to pay for whatever;
It is you have or have not saved and
If you don't mind baby-
I'd rather help us both avoid an emotional grave
Oh yes!
I said US because you stepped to me like Big Daddy
Talking bout Aw Aw girl-
in me you can trust;
so it's a must that you take this loan serious

I am yours in an earthly sense
True asset of the father's business;
so witness the intensity on my face
Whatever you withdraw from me;
It must be replaced with deposits-
that are beyond equal

See I remember those CDs-
Constantly Depleting accounts-
of past women that left you
with a statement that read-
No Funds Available
Then I came along and made you again sailable-
with a love that was unfailable;
so do not mismanage this account

I am your maximizer account
sent from He who in 3 days rose
More precious than gold . . .
Not a digger

I just need to know if you can afford the interest
of your interest;
In me as a permanent love interest
and I want to make sure you understand the details
of this contracted commitment
No intention on hitting you with excess fees
of intimidating prose
So let me break it down for you baby
In plain terms
If you fuck up this account-
It will forever be closed

The Pursuit of Prominence

The pursuit of prominence
The imagery of the one on top-
May not be testosterone dominant
Traditionally men were out trying to-
Divide spirits and conquer pussy;
With higher scores of acquiring pussies
than former pussies
Could this just be role reversal?
Or has the devil tapped into a new way to-
Fuck us all up universal
Rehearsals of funerals of young corpses;
All cause those on the front lines lived an example-
That had their minds warped
What's really going on here?
From Boys to Men, no longer leading from the front;
But opting for the rear
Are firemen pole dancing at their stations;
Or are cops cross dressing in drag so that-
From some childhood pain,
they can take a vacation?
Are there pussies in the Capitol
reporting to other cocks-
With their hands on the buttons of our life's X-Box?
Are there broken wrists in surgery
not wanting to be fixed
Are there teachers passing out A's to the little ones-
Who have similar sticks they can lick?
Are there gang bangers
harder than the sidewalk itself;
Throwing up signs but show no signs of-
Understanding that in the beginning, they were—

Given so much wealth?
My words may make you angry and
You may wish for them to die;
But I have to speak God's truth
That says your homosexual lifestyle is a lie
I'm not even gone front like
I'm even close to sin free
I'm just wondering who can show me
where in the Bible,
God created Adam and Steve
You outgoing and flamboyant gay men-
I actually have respect for you-
Cause at least no one has to guess
what's up with you
But you Down Low men make my stomach turn
Talking about "I'm not gay,
I just like having sex with other men"
And when your wives test positive for AIDS,
to them, and your children,
A new life you can't lend
If your sleeping preference was so innocent then-
Why do it in the dark?
Cause you're to much of a coward
to face the sunlight
Whenever you play that part
Go ahead and be whomever's private dancer
But you're setting a twisted example for the-
boys coming up behind you and
for that, in the end, you will have to answer

He's Just A Man

You heard him say "Yes we can"!
But you forgot, he's just a man
You look to him to be the worker of your miracles;
cause you removed from your life,
the head of all things spiritual
I believe he puts on his pants one leg at a time-
just like regular men do-
but when the "Great Black Hope"
isn't doing what you feel he should;
you change your vote to white and say I'm thru
You heard him say "Yes we can"! and
though that was a promise made by him alone;
he was speaking of a collective effort that would-
bring change if everyone
got in their perspective zone
You heard him say "Yes we can"!
So I guess the mess that his predecessor left
is in his mighty hands
Daily he faces immeasurable stress-
from the world's demands
It would be no surprise if his hope-
began to sink like sand
He threw out his rod of charm
and many fish he caught
And the color of his skin was a selling point;
by which massive votes were bought
Yet in the doctor's office his chart
could mirror that of you or the man in your house
This man still has to take care of his 2 daughters
and find time to romance his spouse

Hold him to his word as in sincerity and truth;
it should've been given-
but don't get it twisted-
He too has to rely on God to get him thru-
his accomplishments and failures, while he is living
He's got the whole world in his hands is a song I
believe is about the owner of the highest resident
Not the polished (here's our 40 acres and a mule) 44th President
It's evident
We're wading through these times of recession;
but slow your roll and unto the Lord give a loud Shabak!

Understanding that through Christ
you can do ALL things
Not through President Barack

Public Announcement

Like a woman basking in the pride of the acrobats
and accolades of her pussy
Note: My shit is good
Fierce tongue firing up mental erections
and spilling over orgasms of oral lava
You think what I say but really never would
Could you kindly get a mop so no one slips-
on the mouths that have dropped
You seek to put me in a box and
make me someone I'm not-
Cause the money for your fantasy of "them"
you sadly aint got
Word Play powerful like an espresso-
from the Coffee Bean
You've never heard me feature so-
you don't know why rare I am deemed
The doggy styled life of reality I took-
so later I could share
You can close your eyes tighter but-
the facts are still there
I aim to get bare and come from behind-
your perception's curtain
Poetry is a gift within itself-
demanding acceptance of its truth,
that's for certain
Worth you can't place on me with a mere tag
When the Master created me-
He let His best kept secret out of the bag
I can eat crepes with the Obama's-
or ribs with folks in the hood
My words are packaged for delivery universal-
not ordinary

Note: My shit is good
Poems are too long you declare but-
would you say that If I was a dick or a vacation
Not for those of short attention span-
as it breathes of deep revelations
I've come to understand that;
you have to let haters feed you
not slow speed you
For this here art form I'd even bleed
My pen is the umbilical cord for-
every word that is my seed
Don't need your seal of approval
The burning in my belly to eat of it-
is the only necessary creed
I'm taking the lead
Note: My shit is good
Contents thereof you can't live without
Fake ass connoisseurs keep printing headlines-
to make others doubt it
But I just re-route it—
cause for the essence of this expression;
I'm the EXTRA
and now you can read all about it
Cloud it . . . . NO
Broke through them with a new one
and brought out the sunshine
No matter how old I am to date
keep getting "mo betta" like fine wine
Extensive vocal data base matching up with-
other prophets with like minds
Grind is ridiculous-
continuing shifts in my sleep
I'll let this cerebral fuck stop
and give you a chance for some relief

I Am

I may not be your vision of beauty;
so it must've been quite a shock when-
you got rejected while offering my man the booty
Truly committed to me as we are-
intertwined in a divine unity;
not just a lets see how things go situation-
Perhaps you could find something similar if-
you would move your mind past mere penetration
Spiritual News Flash or much needed revelation
I Am a sight for deeper eyes because my wise-
is more seductive than my thighs;
Examine my shoulder and you'll see a slide show-
of where my man's joy resides and his problems die

I may not be your vision of that which-
would cause a man to think about sex,
but let me clear up that which has you perplexed;
by unveiling the fact that within me-
all that is complex is a turn on as my man's mind-
is encouraged to stretch;
which is a desired outcome of those who-
have indulged in the simplicity of open legs
See with you a man is left to ask-
how long have you been open or
what time do you close?
As if you were a store of convenience;
but my man is genius and knows good business-
so he would never give up his asset for a liability
I give him the love of a God sent trilogy . . .
Me . . . Myself . . . and . . . I
although you don't understand why-
just know that . . . . .I Am . . . .

I Am the woman who won't have to-
resort to juvenile exchanges of vocal competitions;
to prove myself
Nor will I be your challenger in the next-
ghetto spelling bee in which I win the title-
by proudly looking at the observant judges
aka instigators;
as I answer Bitch, **originating from** the hoods of
Los Angeles, **meaning** a woman who is trifling-
used in a sentence-The Bitch was trying to
fuck my man!
Proper Spelling—B-I-T-C-H—Bitch!
No I Am not the woman who will do that because unlike you,
I am not operating under a false sense of self-worth.
All and Real Woman . . .
His Woman . . .
I Am

TRUST

Something that's a real mutha fucka is Trust
You gradually give it away
And yet it leaves you abrupt and
have you drinking from the drips of your own blood
Wounds leaking with deception-
of the one who said it was you they loved
Security pulled up from under you like
that of a mis-positioned rug

Slug from the imaginary bullet within your heart
as you try to bypass the pain from the woman
you deemed Queen
yet she successfully tore you apart,
with her infidelities, wrapped with a warm smile
Had you fooled for a good while

Child gets on the school bus and to you they wave
Never knowing that they would be taken on a detour that would
forever detour their child like ways

Stayed in an abusive cycle too long
Find yourself at the steps of a shelter, reminiscing
On when you stood before family and friends
and took vows for a happy home
Now as the door opens with a stranger's greeting
You ask yourself where did I go wrong
Songs changed on your station
as you never imagined
this hells creation that you need to blame
on someone . . . . so
Why not the producer of creation
But was He trusted before your pains declaration
True revelation

In who do we trust
The answer to this question is a must
See cause there's something
that's a real mutha fucka
and it's name is Trust
You give it no degree to earn
Until you wake up and feel its betrayals burns

Yearning for a companion other than those under 10
You promised that you were different than
all my other men
Suddenly (at least I thought)
you began to verbalize my intellect
till it lowered its sense that used to be common
Now in common are my past and present bruises
Same drug
Just a different method to use it

Walked up to the park bench where
everyone was gathering for the office potluck
Just my luck
I got a front row seat
To you and my other 'girlz' tearing down me
Chance to see what's real between us, in 3D
Yes, I watched the 3 of you
(Dishonest, Dirty, and Dangerous)
discuss, about me, your true views

Sitting in the pews
Receiving counseling with my wife
couldn't help but notice you always seemed
a bit contrite
I guess the cloth you allow to be your cover
was starting to smother you with the depth
of your sin
In the light you were teaching me
how to improve my marriage
But in the dark, you and my wife were joining skins

There's something that's a real mutha fucka
and it's name is Trust
Eat this reality's whole slice of bread
don't just nibble on the crust
Trust is something you freely give
But there is something that you were freely given
Start to rely on that
and a different way you can be livin
Take your 'GUT' from the back and
place it on the front lines
I tell you
whenever I felt it-
it was right on time
It lets you know that something just aint right
Especially when it wont allow you to get rest at night
It speaks thru the Holy Spirit
or from experience of things that previously hit you
It makes you uncomfortable
so you can look at a situation clearly
and know what to do
It's something that we feel to our core
Listen to your Gut and learn
To Trust yourself more

Came To Say Good Bye

To all those whose mission was to have me live a lie
I'm not here to trip, I just came to say good bye
You used to have my present tense on lock but
I've been released from what's past so your-
Concentration Camp will be transferred to a pine box
On my good sense you had me rolling over-
like a rover that lost its range
Strange is the fact that I knew a better me
had to exist but
my mental strength was broken
like a flipped man's wrist
Now thick like grits is my skin
No more collaborations of now and then
Sure, troubles may come in a different form
But the weather is changing as I
break the sun out on all past storms;
that once had my spirit torn-
now exchanged for other norms
I remember when my soul was turning tricks
against God-
for any Rod whose "staff" would comfort me . . .
so unfree to be-
the stand up woman to whom-
the master paid the highest fee
It's hard to get up when you've laid down for so long
My esteem was working the sunset strip
like clockwork
I didn't know how to sing a new song
Rape, verbal abuse, homelessness or
some other form of degradation

I've pulled into every one of your stations;
with no vacation but-
permanent relief I need
Sly laughter from you who-
packed my picture in your getaway bag;
like you wanted a reminder of how you watched me-
foam at the mouth and bleed with tears that plead
So many wrong seeds planted
as we all take life for granted
Like a deer panted in search of waters not seen
More than seven times fallen but still I rise;
because my father is the King of Kings
Flossing true "bling" as all my filthy stains He cleans and says;
my child you will shine brighter-
cause you've been redeemed
Tears fill my eyes at the end of this part of the race
I started out last, but came up first place
Haste has no control in the plans-
for which God set the route
I gave Him my struggles
and in time He brought me out

Had my taste of strange fruit from my own kind
Jazz scatting the greeting hey girl—
while robbing my trust blind
Found a rumor of my death then ran into me
and almost lost your breath
Yes, you had to pretend you were relieved;
while multitasking to ensure no bones
ran down your sleeves-
cleave to you no more

You were already on your way out;
so see yourself past the door
I thank you for any kindness you showed me
once upon a time;
so I feel no need to even a score
God said for me there's more
and more of me there'll be
In hind sight I realize that
you may have helped set me free
So glee is the new club I've joined
"You are not what happened to you"
is the new phrase I've coined
Loins filled with possibilities of
the impossible, through Him, which all things are
By grace I've come this far
Not an image of mediocrity
But the face of the new bar
Through trials access granted, not denied
And in case you're confused,
you can't purchase a ticket to the next ride

Now I enter the cemetery in search of plots for-
all the relationships I must bury
Feelings breed great emotion but don't vary
Carry my bullet proof vest full of holes-
as I move forward to accept my blessings
Promised by God after I learned
my intended lessons
Keep those who have your back at post
and all others close
When in doubt get on your knees not as prey,
but to be heard-
by He who can give you the most
Stop sharing permanent things-
with people who temporarily reside
And with that said . . .
Bullshit . . . .
to you and all your relatives-
I came to say goodbye

Excuse Me

Excuse me while I fall in love with myself
Excuse me while I clean all your bullshit
off my mental shelf
Excuse me while I get perception
that is much clearer
Excuse me while I tell abuse "Hell No"
as it tries to get nearer
Excuse me while I look at my past and just let go
Excuse me while I change the flavor of my flow
Excuse me while I exercise my liberty and
Speak Out Loud
Excuse me while I take the chains off my inner child
Excuse me while I pamper myself first class style
Excuse me while I get over my fears
Excuse me while I embrace
ALL this SEXY right here
Excuse me while I give myself a compliment
Excuse me while I clear a path for all that is
Heaven sent
Excuse me while I turn down your invitation-
for a dance in the dark
Excuse me while I choose a REAL man
to play the next part
Excuse me while I enjoy spending time even alone
Excuse me as I escort ALL that is not of God-
out of my priority zone
Excuse me for staring at myself that is so damn fine
Excuse me for choosing to get drunk off His spirit
and bypass the wine

Excuse me as I keep praying for the compassion to-
forgive me and you
Excuse me for still living when-
you thought your unthinkable acts
would deem me thru
Excuse me while I release a genuine laugh
Excuse me for walking by slow BUT-
I didn't want you haters to miss the chance to-
Kiss-
My-
Ass!

Sequel Sneak Peak
Soul's Man

.... Imperfectly perfect
Showed up when I had discontinued my search for
The beauty of a lifetime dinner for two
When fears from my past want to push you away
It's just something that your patience
won't allow me to do
So in tune with me
You know what I'm feeling without my revealing
You're keen to my need for a 'fix' of confidence
as trust is a mantle that I've handed
to the wrong men .... Way back when
When you're present I can join the night in rest
You cover me with protection and provision
not that which creates a need for makeup's best
Our rendezvous are so surreal
Feels like I'm in a strange land
Thank you cards go out to the creator
Cause you're my soul's man ....

I Love You Corey

THE END

Credits

Leading Man-   God

Leading Lady-   Duania Hall

Photography-   Light It Up Photography
Corey (my man) Henderson

Cover-   DEZIGNS II
Darnell Loper

Model-   Duania Hall

Wardrobe-   Duania Hall

Hair-   Enawe Hair Studio
Darise (my girl) Sanker

Makeup-   MAC
Janay Van Sylk

Supporting Cast-   Family
Friends
Lovers
Haters
Abusers
Back Stabbers

Thank you for sharing this part of me. I hope you were not only entertained but encouraged, enlightened, and elevated. I love you with the love of God. Peace and Blessings.

I am a poet, event host, and motivational speaker. If you would like to book me for your special event contact me at rootsofdsoul@yahoo.com or bossin39@me.com